SAVVY INTERVIEWING

Books & CD-ROMs by Drs. Caryl and Ron Krannich

101 Dynamite Answers to Interview Questions
101 Secrets of Highly Effective Speakers
201 Dynamite Job Search Letters
Best Jobs For the 21st Century
Change Your Job, Change Your Life
The Complete Guide to International Jobs and Careers
The Complete Guide to Public Employment
The Directory of Federal Jobs and Employers
Discover the Best Jobs for You!
Dynamite Cover Letters
Dynamite Networking For Dynamite Jobs
Dynamite Resumes
Dynamite Salary Negotiations
Dynamite Tele-Search
The Educator's Guide to Alternative Jobs and Careers
Find a Federal Job Fast!
From Air Force Blue to Corporate Gray
From Army Green to Corporate Gray
From Navy Blue to Corporate Gray
Get a Raise in 7 Days
High Impact Resumes and Letters
International Jobs Directory
Interview For Success
Job-Power Source CD-ROM
Jobs and Careers With Nonprofit Organizations
Jobs For People Who Love to Travel
Mayors and Managers
Moving Out of Education
Moving Out of Government
The Politics of Family Planning Policy
Re-Careering in Turbulent Times
Resumes & Job Search Letters For Transitioning Military Personnel
Savvy Interviewing
Savvy Resume Writer
Shopping the Exotic South Pacific
Treasures and Pleasures of Australia
Treasures and Pleasures of China
Treasures and Pleasures of Hong Kong
Treasures and Pleasures of India
Treasures and Pleasures of Indonesia
Treasures and Pleasures of Italy
Treasures and Pleasures of Paris and the French Riviera
Treasures and Pleasures of Singapore and Bali
Treasures and Pleasures of Thailand
Ultimate Job Source CD-ROM

Savvy Interviewing
The Nonverbal Advantage

Caryl Rae Krannich
Ronald L. Krannich

IMPACT PUBLICATIONS
Manassas Park, Virginia

Liability/Warranty: The author and publisher have made every attempt to provide the reader with accurate information. However, given constant changes in the employment field, they make no claims that this information will remain accurate at the time of reading. Furthermore, this information is presented for information purposes only. The author and publisher make no claims that using this information will guarantee the reader a job. The author and publisher shall not be liable for any loss or damages incurred in the process of following the advice presented in this book.

Library of Congress Cataloging-in-Publication Data

Krannich, Caryl Rae
  Savvy interviewing: the nonverbal advantage / Caryl Rae
Krannich, Ronald L. Krannich
    p. cm.—(The career savvy series)
  Includes bibliographical references and index.
  ISBN 1-57023-123-0
    1. Employment interviewing. 2. Nonverbal communication. 3.
Body language. I. Krannich, Ronald L. II. Title. III. Series.

HF5549.5.I6 K723 1999
650.14—dc21

                        99-052712

Publisher: For information on Impact Publications, including current and forthcoming publications, authors, press kits, bookstore, and submission requirements, visit Impact's Web site: *www.impactpublications.com*

Publicity/Rights: For information on publicity, author interviews, and subsidiary rights, contact the Public Relations and Marketing Department: Tel. 703/361-7300 or Fax 703/335-9486.

Sales/Distribution: Bookstore sales are handled through Impact's trade distributor: National Book Network, 15200 NBN Way, Blue Ridge Summit, PA 17214, Tel. 1-800-462-6420. All other sales and distribution inquiries should be directed to the publisher: Sales Department, IMPACT PUBLICATIONS, 9104 Manassas Dr., Suite N, Manassas Park, VA 20111-5211, Tel. 703/361-7300, Fax 703/335-9486, or *careersavvy@impactpublications.com*

Book design by Kristina Ackley

Contents

Interviews in Your Future   1

Preoccupied With the Verbal 1
Job Interview Decisions 2
K,S,Q + VIQ + NVI = Successful Outcome 4
The Performance Interview: Understanding and
    Influencing a Decision 5
What is Your NVIQ? 5
Advance Your Future 10

The Nonverbal Advantage   11

What is Nonverbal Communication? 12
Why Are Nonverbal Messages Important? 13
How Do Nonverbal Behaviors Affect
    the Interview Outcome? 16

Nonverbal Behavior in
Different Interview Settings   20

The Telephone Interview 20
Nonverbal Behaviors in the Telephone Interview 22
The Videoconference Interview 23
Nonverbal Behaviors in the Videoconference Interview 25
The Face-To-Face Interview 26
Nonverbal Behaviors in the Face-To-Face Interview 27

Take Advantage of Your Best Image   28

You Want to Fit in—Not Stand Out 29
Good Grooming Pays: Men 31
Dress to Your Highest Potential: Men 34
Your Extra Edge—Your Personal Coloring is Key: Men 42

Identify Your Color Type: Men 43

Maximize Your Look of Competence: Men 45

Good Grooming Pays: Women 46

Dress To Your Highest Potential: Women 53

Your Extra Edge—Your Personal Coloring is Key: Women .. 60

Identify Your Color Type: Women 61

Maximize Your Look of Competence: Women 63

Space and Time: Two-Way Messages   65

Personal Space and Conversational Distance 66

Seating Choices 70

Conversational Space 72

Cultural Differences and Personal Space 73

Read the Interviewer's Cues— 74

Use Space to Your Advantage 74

Make Time Your Ally.. 75

Make Your Body Language Speak Superlatives   77

Nonverbal Behaviors That Regulate Interaction 78

Communicate Positive Attitudes 80

Avoid Communicating Messages of Deception 83

Put Your Best Foot Forward 86

Synchronize Your Body Movements
With the Interviewer's... 87

The Eyes Have It: Make Facial Expression Work For You   89

Convey Appropriate Facial Expression 89

Positive Eye Contact... 93

Your Face And Eyes Convey Powerful Messages.................... 95

Your Winning Vocal Advantage 97

Project Your Voice: Project Your Competence 98
Pitch Patterns Speak For You 100
Convey Your Competence With
  a Controlled, Confident Pace 102
Don't Let Nonfluencies Weaken Your Credibility 103
Avoid Poor Diction—A Credibility Robber 106
Put Them All Together and You're Dynamic 108

Don't Be Afraid of Silence 109

Don't Jump In Too Soon or Talk Too Much 109
Focused Silence in Salary Negotiations Can Add $$$ 111

Put It All Together:
You've Got Everything to Gain 113

Behaviors To Live By Every Day 114
Behaviors To Avoid 116
Psych Yourself for Your Interview 119

About the Authors 122

Index 124

PREFACE

Much has been written about preparing for interviews. Taken as a whole, interview books primarily focus on the job applicant—how to become a savvy interviewee. They provide advice on developing various interview skills, such as researching jobs and employers; conducting informational interviews; determining strategies for responding to questions; developing responses to specific questions, formulating questions about the organization, the job and the other employees; negotiating terms of employment; and following up on interviews. In fact, we've contributed to this literature by authoring two interview books: *Interview For Success* and *101 Dynamite Answers to Interview Questions*.

Most experts on job interviews examine the "do's" and "don'ts" of the verbal interchange between the applicant and the employer. Not surprisingly, most people believe they communicate primarily through the words they use. However, communication studies reveal that only about 7 percent of communication takes place through the verbal channel. In fact, over 90 percent of the message is communicated nonverbally! If interviewees concentrate only on their verbal communication, they overlook the major nonverbal channels they are using to communicate. Whether they realize it or not, they communicate numerous messages nonverbally. Unaware of their nonverbal communication, they convey messages by default rather than with a sense of positive purpose.

This book focuses on nonverbal messages interviewees convey in interviews. We use examples from the employment interview and the performance appraisal interview since those are the two interviews most frequently encountered in one's work life. However, the channels of communication—from appearance and dress to body language, facial expression, and the use of space, silence and voice—all convey messages to the interviewer. While the job applicant may give good verbal responses to questions, contradictory nonverbal behaviors may cost him the job!

Recognition of and attention to nonverbal communication behaviors and the messages they convey are important and applicable to everyday interactions with people. In fact, if you practice them in everyday life, you will carry them into the interview with you—naturally.

Although the information in this book primarily relates to nonverbal messages interviewees convey to interviewers, the principles can and should be applied to reading the nonverbal behaviors and hence the messages conveyed by the interviewer.

Through much of the book, "he" is the pronoun of choice. To use s/he, or to keep switching back and forth from one to the other, unnecessarily interferes with ease of reading. The use of "he" in no way suggests that the skills discussed are a male domain. The female author of this book is comfortable with this usage, and assures the reader that some of the best interviewees we have encountered are women!

Employers, especially those who conduct screening interviews, indicate they often make a decision about a potential employee—positive or negative—within the first three minutes of an interview. Make sure your nonverbal behaviors during those first three minutes—as well as the rest of your life—convey positive messages about both your professional and personal competence!

SAVVY INTERVIEWING

1

Interviews in Your Future

An interview! The very thought makes otherwise savvy people feel somewhat uneasy and apprehensive. And if the interview is scheduled within a day or two, it could produce physiological signs of nervous apprehension—tummy butterflies, a dry mouth or moist palms. Indeed, many of us become nervous at the prospect of an interview simply because we realize how important it is to our future. Whether we're a job applicant or meeting our boss for an annual performance review, we know our future is on the line. For better or for worse, this interview can change our future. With so much at stake, who wouldn't at least feel the excitement of a little nervous anticipation?

Preoccupied With the Verbal

But how do you prepare for the interview? Do you try to anticipate questions and then develop appropriate answers? Maybe you develop a list of thoughtful questions you should ask at the interview. Except for deciding what to wear and knowing the importance of a firm handshake and nice smile, most people prepare for an interview by focusing almost solely on the verbal interchange—what they should say. Accordingly, little attention gets paid to nonverbal messages—critical communication that often dominates the interview as well as determines interview outcomes.

Job Interview Decisions

Interview decisions do affect our lives. As the interviewer, an employer has several decision options:

1. Invite the applicant back for another interview.
2. Offer the applicant the job for which he interviewed.
3. Reject the applicant as not being a good fit for the job.
4. Decide to postpone the decision altogether.

Another possible, and sometimes unexpected, outcome is to consider the applicant for another position within the organization. So the candidate may get a job offer after all—but for an entirely different position!

But the interviewer isn't the only person participating in the interview, and he is not the only person who makes a critical decision. While the job applicant provides information—both verbally and nonverbally—to the employer, this applicant also has to make important decisions. For example, is he really interested in working for this company? Does he like the position for which he is interviewing?

No matter how much the applicant has researched the organization, no matter how much information has been amassed, no matter how great the offer—if one is made, in the end, much of the applicant's decision is based on how well he feels he will "fit in" and be happy with the company. This *gut reaction* is based almost entirely on nonverbal cues picked up during the interview. Some of the nonverbal cues are perceived on a conscious level; our job applicant might be able to verbalize them. Other cues are perceived on a subliminal level; he is not even able to verbalize to himself what they are. *"It just feels right,"* he might say. *"I think I will fit in."*

Much the same, of course, can be said of the interviewer in this situation. No matter how much information he has on paper about the applicant prior to the interview, he needs to meet with him face-to face to determine if, indeed, he

> Much of the applicant's decision is based on how he feels he will "fit in" and be happy with the company. This *gut reaction* is based almost entirely on nonverbal cues picked up during the interview.

is fully qualified. We have heard applicants, who thought they were eminently qualified for a position, and who also thought they should be shoe-ins for the job, make joking references to friends that the interviewer must want to interview them in person to see whether they have two heads! They failed to realize that despite their many paper qualifications, their interpersonal skills were also critical elements to the hiring process. How well they would fit into the organization would be determined by both their verbal and nonverbal behavior.

Since the interviewer already has a great deal of information on the candidate prior to the interview, we can assume the candidate is qualified in terms of knowledge, skills and experience. All candidates who are invited to be interviewed have the prerequisite paper qualifications. At this point, the crucial test centers on nonverbal interaction and possible cues this interaction provides for assessing one's professional and personal "fitness" for the job. How well does the interviewer like you? How well does he think you will fit into the organizational culture, interact with your superiors, manage your subordinates and handle clients? How long will you stay with the organization? Will you be loyal to the company? Can you be trusted? Will you be happy working there?

K,S,Q + VIQ + NVI = Successful Outcome

Your Knowledge, plus your Skills, plus your Qualifications form the basis for a successful outcome. No matter how savvy your verbal and nonverbal skills, if you do not have the basic qualifications to perform the job, you are unlikely to even be invited to the interview, and less likely to be offered the job.

However, many well-qualified people, qualified in terms of the skill requirements, don't do well in the interview. They are unable to respond in a positive way to the verbal interchange of the interview. As suggested in the second part of our equation, having foundation skills is not enough; the candidate must successfully communicate his abilities in the interview. So the VIQ refers to one's Verbal Interview Quotient—the ability to reassure the interviewer that the applicant does indeed possess the ability to do the job as well as to ask the questions that will allow him to decide whether he wants the job.

We discuss the verbal aspects of interviewing in two of our other books: *Interview for Success* and *101 Dynamite Answers to Interview Questions.* In this book we are primarily concerned with the NVIQ—your nonverbal interview quotient. As we will see in the next chapter, this often neglected aspect of the interview may be the most critical to receiving a job offer!

The Performance Interview: Understanding and Influencing a Decision

By the time you find yourself in a performance review, your supervisor has probably already reached conclusions about your performance. Some supervisors arrive at a decision and then schedule the interview merely to inform the employee where he stands. Other managers conduct a performance review that allows greater give-and-take; the outcome will be influenced by the content and quality of the interchange. Obviously, the second situation is preferable to the employee who prefers having input that can affect the outcome of the interview. But in both situations, the employee's verbal and nonverbal communication can affect the outcome of the performance interview.

If the employee perceives that the results of the review have been predetermined and his role is to meekly sit, listen, and nod his head in agreement with everything said, then he has both verbally and nonverbally acquiesced to this one-way flow of communication; the outcome is sealed. If, however, the employee understands that this can be a two-way communication flow and he can affect the outcome, then he can participate in the decision-making process.

What is Your NVIQ?

Do you know how to manage your nonverbal behaviors so that the messages you communicate are those you wish others to consciously and subconsciously perceive? The following questions will give you a chance to test your Nonverbal Interview Quotient. As you respond to each question, take time to consider not only whether you are answering in the affirmative or negative. If you agree, consider what might be an appropriate behavior for the situation, and then check your response against the behavior suggested in later chapters. If you disagree but do not know what your behavior should be, you will find related information in the following chapters.

Your NVIQ (Nonverbal Interview Quotient)

Respond to each of the following statements by circling the number at right which best represents your situation.

Scale: 1 = strongly disagree   4 = agree
        2 = disagree   5 = strongly agree
        3 = maybe, not certain

1. I understand that nonverbal cues can   1 2 3 4 5
   influence the outcome of an interview
   to a greater extent than the words ex-
   changed.

2. I know how to make my selection of   1 2 3 4 5
   clothing and grooming choices work
   for me and my goal in the interview.

3. I know how to project positive non-verbal statements as I greet the receptionist.   1 2 3 4 5

4. While sitting in the reception area waiting to meet the interviewer, I try to find materials about the company to read.   1 2 3 4 5

5. When the interviewer approaches me, I stand up with a smile and extend my hand to shake hers.   1 2 3 4 5

                                                                                     1 2 3 4 5

6. I know how to "read" the physical environment where the interview takes place and utilize these elements to my advantage.

7. I know how to enter the interview space and what to do there.   1 2 3 4 5

8. I wait for the interviewer to indicate where I should be seated.   1 2 3 4 5

9. I know how to best sit during the interview.   1 2 3 4 5

10. I know what facial expressions are appropriate during the interview.   1 2 3 4 5

11. I keep my hands in my lap during the interview except when gesturing.   1 2 3 4 5

12. I avoid folding my arms across my chest during the interview.   1 2 3 4 5

13. I walk and sit with my head erect.   1 2 3 4 5

14. I smile pleasantly in a professional manner.   1 2 3 4 5

15. I know where to look—focus my gaze—during the interview.   1 2 3 4 5

16. I keep my feet flat on the floor during an interview.   1 2 3 4 5

17. I vary my vocal inflections as I ask and answer questions   1 2 3 4 5

18. I know what degree of projection— loudness—I should use as I talk.   1 2 3 4 5

19. I know what pace of speaking I should use during the interview.   1 2 3 4 5

20. I have very few, if any, vocalized pauses as I talk.   1 2 3 4 5

21. I know what to do during silent spaces.   1 2 3 4 5

22. I know how to behave so as to communicate consistent messages between my verbal and nonverbal cues.   1 2 3 4 5

23. I know how much to say.   1 2 3 4 5

24. I know how to project dynamism during the interview.   1 2 3 4 5

25. I know how to be perceived—through nonverbal behaviors—as being knowledgeable and competent.   1 2 3 4 5

TOTAL

Compute and Interpret Your Score

Add the values of the numbers you circled. The highest possible score is 125—this would be your score if every number you circled was a 5. If your score is over 100, and if the behaviors you would engage in are indeed good choices, congratulations, you are well on your way to positive nonverbal communication. However, you will want to check as you read the chapter that follow, to determine whether the nonverbal behaviors you would engage in are ones that best promote your goals in your interview situations. If your composite score is 75 or less, you will want to read the following chapters with a careful eye to discerning the variety of non-verbal behaviors and how they are likely to be interpreted by the interviewer.

Advance Your Future

During your lifetime, you will participate in many interviews. Some will have a greater impact on your future than others, but all will affect your life in either positive or negative ways. No doubt you are aware that your verbal interchange will affect the outcome of the interview. But maybe you haven't given much thought, except that you should dress neatly and smile as you greet the interviewer, as to how your nonverbal interchange might affect the outcome. Moreover, you probably haven't considered how you can manage your nonverbal behaviors to exert a positive influence on the interchange.

> **Before you ever open your mouth to speak in an interview, the other person has perceived volumes and made judgments. You can make your nonverbal behaviors work for you in ways more powerful than your words.**

Before you ever open your mouth to speak in an interview, the other person has perceived volumes and made judgments. You can make your nonverbal behaviors work for you in ways that speak more powerfully than your words. Continue with us as we explore how you communicate with words unspoken—how you can wield personal power that affirms your competence.

2

THE NONVERBAL ADVANTAGE

Employers know that job applicants want to make a good impression during the interview. They also know many books and career coaches advise job candidates on how they should best respond to anticipated interview questions as well as what questions they should ask of employers. Since employers know few job seekers will verbally volunteer information about their weaknesses, interviewers look for weaknesses in the manner in which interviewees handle the interview.

Employers also know that people can control their verbal behaviors far more easily than they can control their non-verbal behaviors. The employer realizes that if the verbal and nonverbal behaviors of the applicant are inconsistent, it is the nonverbal behavior that tells the truth. Hence employers, at times intuitively while at other times consciously, place greater weight on the validity of the applicant's nonverbal behavior.

If you manage your nonverbal as well as your verbal behaviors, you have a significant advantage over other applicants who pay attention to their verbal, but neglect their nonverbal communication.

What is Nonverbal Communication?

Nonverbal communication encompasses many types of behaviors. However, for our purposes we focus on major nonverbal elements that affect the outcome of the interview. We will examine those elements over which the interviewee can exert some control, or manage his response to uncontrollable elements in the situation to influence the outcome in a positive manner.

We especially look at how one's physical appearance and dress impact the interviewer. This is usually the first thing perceived by the employer in a face-to-face interview. Even before the candidate says a word, the employer has already begun to form initial impressions that include judgments as to whether this person will fit into the organization and whether he is competent. Employers report forming initial impressions of a candidate so negative they wish they could cancel the interview right then and there, without wasting their time or that of the applicant.

Your body language—how you stand and sit, what you do with your shoulders, arms and hands, how you position your legs and feet and whether they stay still or move nervously around the floor in front of your chair—speaks to the employer.

Your facial expression and eye movements—even pupil dilation—send messages that indicate enthusiasm or disinterest, honesty or deceit, comfortable or uncomfortable, friendly or unfriendly. Some studies suggest that eye cues are the ones we pay the most attention to when forming impressions of others.

Vocal inflection and projection, the most important nonverbal cues for phone interviews and important variables in face-to-face interviews, suggest how confident we feel. These elements can convey enthusiasm versus lack of interest, as well as honesty versus deceit.

How we handle moments of silence, whether we rush to fill the space—sometimes saying too much or conveying verbal information better left unsaid—communicates our ease or unease with the situation.

How we make use of the space in which we find ourselves, especially as it regards the arrangement of furniture—

> Vocal inflection and projection suggest how confident we feel. These elements can convey enthusiasm versus lack of interest, as well as honesty versus deceit. Moments of silence, whether we rush to fill the space, communicate our ease or unease with the situation.

the chair we sit in as the interview takes place, the desk that may come between us and the interviewer as well as personal space—may work for or against us.

Why Are Nonverbal Messages Important?

Most people mistakenly believe they primarily communicate through they words they use. But communication studies consistently report that over 90 percent of communication takes place through nonverbal channels. Most estimates suggest that only about 7 percent of one's message is communicated verbally. Approximately 38 percent of one's message is communicated through vocal characteristics, and 55 percent through body language. Your appearance, the vocal inflections you use, your body language—all convey messages to the people around you. Even though many of us initially may not like the fact that nonverbal messages play such an important role in the information we convey to others and the impressions they form of us, it is an important function of nonverbal communication. It allows people to form rapid impressions of one another—we about others and they about us. This serves useful functions in society. We rapidly assess whether we should fear danger from another individual in certain settings. We make initial decisions about whether we want to invest more of our time in interaction with an individual we encounter. First impressions influence our lives—both the impression of others which we form, and the impressions they form of us—far more than most of us realize.

Employers who conduct screening interviews in face-to-face settings indicate that, more often than not, they make an initial determination as to whether they will invite the applicant back for further interviews within the first 5 minutes of the interview—some interviewers indicate that 3 minutes is the norm. Further, employers indicate that even though the actual interview may take 30 or 40 minutes, a negative first impression, once formed, rarely changes. It is more likely that an initial positive impression may change to a negative one over the course of the interview! Now you may ask yourself, what is the interviewer able to determine in so little time? What is he responding to? The answer should be apparent. The interviewer responds to first impressions: to the physical appearance/dress of the applicant and to "gut level" reaction that, "I don't like this person," or "I don't feel comfortable with this person." In 3-5 minutes the interviewer hasn't had time to respond to the skill qualifications of the applicant.

You may complain, "that's not fair. The applicant should be judged on his ability to do the job." But that's a rather naive reaction. First, the ability to fit into the workplace is considered a prerequisite for most jobs. The ability to interact easily with the boss, co-workers and clients is considered integral to most jobs. Second, it is a fact that we all make judgments based on initial impressions. We may not all make hiring decisions based on these impressions, and many of us may be open-minded to changing our opinions when other data proves our first impressions wrong. But if we are going to take charge and make our nonverbal behaviors work for us rather than defaulting to behaviors that may be counterproductive to our goals, then like it or not, we may as well recognize that this is the way the world out there works. Once we accept reality, however flawed, we can become more savvy in our nonverbal behaviors.

Nonverbal behaviors are also important because employers know that such behavior is more difficult to control than verbal behavior. Thus, if the two messages are inconsistent, the nonverbal message is the one that is believed. For example, if an applicant is asked why he wants to work for XYZ Company, he may have anticipated this question and carefully planned the strategy behind the way he will respond. He has researched the organization and knows what he thinks they want to hear and he can verbally respond with a well-conceived answer. However, what may trip him up are his nonverbal responses. His vocal inflections may not echo the enthusiasm he has put into the verbal response. He may fail to look the interviewer in the eye, fidget or exhibit other mannerisms that the interviewer perceives as indicating he is being less than honest. He may say all the right things verbally, but his nonverbal behaviors may sabotage his well laid plans.

How Do Nonverbal Behaviors Affect the Interview Outcome?

We know that nonverbal behaviors operate and affect peoples' perceptions—and hence outcomes—in all situations. However, the nonverbal cues are most significant when the individuals involved have little information about the other person. A job interview usually involves people who fit precisely in this category. The employer usually has a piece of paper—the applicant's resume. (The resume also conveys nonverbal cues—the quality and color of paper used as well as the neatness of the copy and use of correct grammar and spelling reflect on the attention to detail the applicant is likely to exhibit on the job.)

> Nonverbal cues are most significant when the individuals involved have little information about the other person. In a job interview, idiosyncrasies of behavior that might go unnoticed by a close acquaintance might send messages that raise red flags.

Other than the information contained on the resume, the interviewer may know nothing about the applicant. So idiosyncrasies of behavior that might go unnoticed by a close acquaintance who was used to his friend's behavior might irritate the interviewer or simply send messages that raise red flags. An individual who lowers his eyes and avoids eye contact may have been raised to believe that lowering one's eyes is a sign of respect. But the employer may view this as a sign of dishonesty. We even have common sayings such as, "He couldn't look me in the eye," or "He had shifty eyes," that indicate how we tend to perceive such behavior in our culture.

The interviewer may view an applicant's behaviors as ingratiating, indicating he is too anxious to please and infer that the individual will be a "yes man"—when the employer doesn't want a "yes man". Another's manner may be seen as too casual and the interviewer may infer a disrespectful attitude and decide the job doesn't mean much to the individual. A person who seems overly sensitive may be seen as being difficult to supervise—how will the manager review a person's work if every critical comment brings hurt feelings?

During the hiring process, we can assume that each and every individual invited for an employment interview has demonstrated, on paper, that he has the prerequisite skills and experience that qualify him to do the job. The employer has made an initial selection of candidates based, in large part, and in many instances solely on candidates' resumes. The first piece of data the interviewer will note and assess when he meets the candidate for the interview is his appearance and dress. What will set one applicant apart from another at this stage is how each looks. Do they fit the interviewer's expectations of what the future employee for the open position should look like? In rapid succession other determinations will be made. Does the applicant display the appropriate warmth, eye contact, manner and mannerisms, and a host of other variables that the interviewer will note on both a conscious and subconscious level?

This will all take place in moments. The interviewer and interviewee have already begun to size each other up as they form impressions of each other. As the interviewer begins the initial small talk portion of the interview, don't make the mistake of assuming that the small talk is unimportant to the outcome. Though not directly ascertaining information about your work content abilities, the interviewer is gleaning information that is every bit as important—perhaps more so. The interviewer is getting a feel for how well he likes you and how well you will fit into the organization.

As the interviewer moves from the initial small talk phase of the interview to the more work related questions regarding the applicant's skills and experience, he will seek to confirm his initial impressions of the candidate. If the initial impressions have been negative, the interviewer will be looking for reasons why the applicant should be knocked out of running for the open position. If the initial impressions have been positive, the interviewer will be seeking to validate those initial instincts as well. So there is really no such thing as small talk. Everything that happens in the course of the interview is important. Those seemingly meaningless comments about the weather or whether the applicant had any difficulty finding his way are all part of the tableau. From the moment the interviewer sets eyes on the applicant, the process is set in motion. The very first thing that makes an impression isn't verbal at all. What precedes and accompanies the verbal interaction of the interview sets the stage for how the verbal interaction will be received and processed.

The savvy interviewee recognizes that his nonverbal behaviors communicate more than the verbal responses he gives to interview questions. He also knows that he can become more aware of his nonverbal behaviors and modify those that may be sabotaging his efforts to get ahead—either on the job or as he interviews for a job. By carefully preparing to manage nonverbal cues just as he strategizes the jist of his verbal responses, the applicant can turn his nonverbal messages to his advantage while, at the same time, becoming more attuned to his reception of the nonverbal messages being conveyed by the interviewer.

3

Nonverbal Behavior in Different Interview Settings

Your nonverbal behaviors affect the perceptions of the interviewer and hence the outcome of every interview. Which nonverbal behaviors become most important vary with the interview setting. Let's examine three interview settings and how nonverbal behaviors affect both interactions and outcomes: the telephone interview, the videoconference interview, and the face-to-face interview. The telephone interview and the face-to-face interview are by far the most common interviews. It is unlikely you will participate in a videoconference interview if you are applying exclusively for positions in or close to your place of residence.

The Telephone Interview

Telephone interviews are being used with increasing frequency by employers both to save time and money. Telephone interviews are usually screening interviews. In other words, the telephone interview is most likely used to determine which candidates to invite for a face-to-face interview. Seldom would a candidate be offered the job during or as a result of only a telephone interview.

Like everyone else, employers are busy people. It seems they need more hours a day than they have in order to get their work done. When the tasks of screening resumes and interviewing applicants are added it can be overwhelming. So employers seek ways to make good decisions while taking less time out of their daily schedule.

After going through a stack of resumes, the employer may have 25 or more applicants that look good on paper. To call each one in for a face-to-face interview would consume a great deal of time. Each interview would likely take an hour or more. If only there were a way to sift through the pile of likely candidates and weed out the ones that look good on paper but may not really be a good fit for the position. The answer is the telephone interview. An employer may only take 5-10 minutes on the phone to determine that she does not need to spend any more time with an applicant. It is not likely to be a good fit for either one. If she can weed out two-thirds or more of the initial pile of likely candidates, she now is left with a more manageable 7 or 8 people to bring in for a face-to-face interview. The telephone screening interview has been a significant time-saver for a busy employer.

In some instances there will be a monetary savings as well. If a regional or nationwide search has been conducted many of the candidates will be from another area and there are travel costs to consider. The costs of airfare, lodging and meals for each candidate add yet another expense to the cost of filling the position. This provides an additional incentive to screen out some candidates before they are invited to a face-to-face job interview.

Nonverbal Behaviors in the Telephone Interview

We will assume our participants are using the audio telephone we are all familiar with. As videotelephones become more prevalent, so that they are common both to organizations and individuals, the comments on videoconferencing in the next section would apply. In the case of the telephone interview, paralanguage, the vocal cues of spoken speech, will be most important. Neither participant is able to see how the other is dressed or groomed. So appearance and dress will not directly impact the perceptions of the other. Likewise body language cues will go unobserved as will facial expression.

> In the telephone interview, paralanguage, the vocal cues of spoken speech, will be most important. Even though how one is dressed and groomed cannot be perceived in the telephone setting, it can still impact on how the individual is perceived.

Although these factors will be unobserved by the other participant, it does not necessarily follow that it will have no effect on the interaction. Studies, and perhaps even common sense, suggest that how we dress, for example, can affect our own behavior in ways that influence the interaction. These other behaviors could impact on the interview. For example, the phone rings at 9:00am at the house of Mary Jones. She is still in her bathrobe, her teeth are not yet brushed and her hair is uncombed. When she answers the phone, it is a potential employer calling. Thank heavens this is not a video call!

While it is true the employer cannot see her, Mary herself feels less than professional in her current attire. So as she responds to the employer's questions, she is a bit more flustered than usual and this is translated into vocal hesitancies. Her tone of voice doesn't have the strength of projection that is characteristic of Mary in professional settings, so she seems less confident than usual. Because she feels uncomfortable, her voice does not project the usual warmth to the person on the other end of the telephone line. Mary's appearance and dress have affected how she feels about herself, and she communicates this to the other person through vocal characteristics. So even though how one is dressed and groomed is not actually viewed by the other person in the telephone setting, it can still impact how the individual is perceived. One part of our demeanor affects other aspects and cues in other areas may leak messages that can be readily perceived by the other participant.

If you are the subject of a telephone screening interview, be on your best behavior. First, be wary that you are not inadvertently sending negative messages through your vocal inflections, tone of voice or level of projection. Second, since so many nonverbal cues we normally rely on for cues in face-to-face communication are absent in telephone communication, your telephone vocal cues must carry more of the message you wish to convey. You must make the vocal cues work for us.

This principle is just as important to the interviewer as to the interviewee, and just as important to the employee whose boss calls to check on the progress of an assignment as it is to the applicant for a position!

The Videoconference Interview

Videoconferencing interviews are used for many of the same reasons as the telephone screening interview. They save time and money. For employment interviews they allow the employer to get impressions of the candidate without the expense of flying a candidate in for an interview. Since videoconferencing allows the interviewer to see as well as hear the candidate, it provides more information than a telephone interview. Videoconference interviews are becoming more common and will become more so as the cost of travel—both time and money—become greater and as the cost of videoconferencing drops. As the quality of telephones with video capability improves and the cost drops, we may find them to be as commonplace as audio telephones are today. But for now videoconferencing requires that both participants (or all participants— as it is possible to conduct panel interviews using this technology) have a video camera and compatible software on their computer.

> Videoconferencing is practical, but the situation presents considerations not inherent in other interview settings. Mannerisms that might go unnoticed in a face-to-face setting are magnified. Your every movement is on view and the center of attention.

Nearly half the largest U.S. corporations use videoconferencing to communicate with their offices in various geographical locations. So it is quite possible that you will be a participant in this interview setting at some point as a job applicant or as an employee. With so many corporations using videoconferencing in the daily conduct of their business, it is natural that they see the value of applying this technology to the interview selection process—using it primarily as a screening tool for mid-management and executive candidates. A number of firms now offer facilities for videoconferencing and rent studio time. So the candidate can drive to a videoconferencing studio near his hometown rather than fly across the country in the early stages of the interview process. In the Washington, D.C. Metro area, for example, Kinko's and Sprint have teamed to offer videoconferencing at their business centers. Most companies will still want a final interview(s) in person, but they can save time and money in the early stages of interviewing far-flung applicants using the videoconference, yet have access to more information than is available through the audio telephone interview.

Nonverbal Behaviors in the Videoconference Interview

Videoconferencing is practical, but the situation presents considerations not inherent in other interview settings. We tend to think that video shows us reality—we see the other person as he is and his behaviors as they actually are. Not quite! Mannerisms that might go unnoticed in a face-to-face setting are magnified. There is little allowance for looking around, checking your watch, rubbing one's nose, arranging one's hair or other little grooming habits. Your every movement is on view and the center of attention. When you are interviewing face-to-face, the other participant(s) have everything in the room on which to focus. When looking at a screen, everything else in the room gets ignored and one's full attention focuses on the face and body on the screen. You may recall that presidential candidate, George Bush, was caught on camera checking his watch at one point during the debates. It turned out to be a visual negative, which conveyed messages that stuck in people's minds.

Your grooming and clothing will be noticed to a greater extent than in person. That red dress or red plaid tie can gain so much attention as it "dances" on camera that it is difficult for the listener to focus on your message! Your lack of eye contact with the camera—and hence by extension with the interviewer—makes him perceive you as less than completely open and honest. Your nervous mannerisms only add to the perception that you have something to hide.

Your professional appearance, confident but not cocky mannerisms as evidenced by your body language, facial expression and vocal indicators, must all send positive cues if you expect to be kept in the running for the position.

The Face-To-Face Interview

We are most familiar with the face-to-face interview. The majority of interviews from employment interviews, interviews to report progress on an assignment, to performance interviews—all are most likely to be in person, face-to-face, across a desk or table. For hiring decisions, although telephone or videoconferencing settings may be used for screening in the early stages of elimination, few people are ever hired without a face-to-face interview with someone in the firm. One might say that the phone and video interviews help employers screen most people out of consideration, but the "in person", face-to-face interview is the setting of choice for the final hiring selection.

Nonverbal Behaviors in the Face-To-Face Interview

All of one's nonverbal behaviors are on display in the face-to-face interview. The advantage here is that because all the cues are on display, none are preeminent in importance as are the vocal cues in the telephone setting. Nor are behaviors overly emphasized as they can be in the video setting. However, a greater number and greater variety of cues are on display and they must be consistent with one another as well as with your verbal message. We will look at the variety of nonverbal cues and the many messages they can convey as well as how to make the messages you communicate, powerful positive statements about your competence and likeability. Your nonverbal behaviorsmust compliment your verbal statements. Your nonverbal behaviors must communicate, "I am competent, but not overbearing. I will work well with clients, my supervisor, co-workers, and subordinates. You will like me. I am like you. I fit into the organization."

4

Take Advantage of Your Best Image

The rat and the squirrel are both rodents. One is despised and detested while the other is thought to be cute. Does a furry, upright tail make that much difference? The answer appears to be a resounding "yes". As a present Mitsubishi ad campaign suggests—image makes all the difference.

We are told by social psychologists that most individuals take only 5-20 seconds to make a determination of another person's value. Employers tell us that when they conduct screening interviews in face-to-face settings, they make an initial determination as to whether they will invite the applicant back for another interview within the first 5 minutes of meeting with him or her. Many employers indicate that even less time—3 minutes or even less, is enough time for them to decide, but they have started forming impressions after as few as twenty seconds! What's more, the same employers say that seldom is an initial negative impression changed to a positive enough one that they will change their minds and invite the person for an additional interview.

What can these employers respond to in so little time? Certainly not to the applicant's skills, knowledge and abilities. Employers, like the rest of humankind, are responding to image—

how the candidate looks, sounds, and interacts. Whether we like it or not, we may as well face up to the fact that this is reality—this is how it works. Because only by accepting this truth are we able to turn it to our advantage.

You Want to Fit in—Not Stand Out

Appearance counts and you have to look the part if you want to be perceived as credible. Image is a factor on which people are selected in or out, promoted, or left behind. Are we suggesting that if you dress the part you can compensate for a lack of skills? Certainly not! What we do contend is that if there are two (or more) equally qualified individuals, and one fits the corporate image and the other does not, guess which one is the likely winner. This is valid whether we are talking about the hiring process or the performance appraisal process. The individual who fits the expected image is actually viewed as being the more competent!

Employers, managers, supervisors—whether or not they recognize it and whether or not they will admit to it—feel more comfortable with people whom they believe hold values similar to their own. If you dress in a manner that is appreciably different than the way they dress, or different from other individuals within the organization, you stand out. Your appearance may shout or whisper that you must be different because your appearance is so different, and that makes the interviewer uncomfortable. What will his boss say if he recommends you for the position? What will other employees think? What will the corporation's clients think? Will they be able to get past your appearance? You have put him in an uncomfortable and risky position.

We all carry around our expectations of what we like and expect in others' appearance. If another's appearance is out of sync with our expectations, we are distracted at the least, and that interferes with our concentration on his message. An even worse outcome is that we value the other person's abilities less. We actually lower our evaluation of his competence.

Hiring decisions are based first on emotions, then on judgments related to the applicant's technical qualifications. Supervisors' assessments of one's on-the-job performance are influenced by emotional considerations as well. You were exposed to this fact of life long before you started looking for or started on the job. As a student, didn't you sense that certain teachers had favorites? Wasn't there someone in the class who was teased as being "teacher's pet"? Studies indicate that this was no figment of your imagination—teachers do have favorites! Some are more discreet about showing favoritism than others, but it exists nonetheless.

> Hiring decisions are based first on emotions, then on judgments related to the applicant's technical qualifications. Supervisors' assessments of one's on-the-job performance are influenced by emotional considerations as well.

Bernard Haldane Associates, a career management firm, presents their clients with a list of 20 job interview knockouts—topping the list is poor personal appearance. Your credentials and qualifications are calling cards. They may get you in the door for an interview if your credentials are appropriately conveyed by your resume. Qualifications alone seldom gain the applicant the job.

Groom and dress so that your appearance is not an issue. If your garb becomes the topic of conversation around the office after you have left, you have almost certainly misjudged your audience and will have lost the battle. If your appearance becomes an issue, it will almost certainly be a knockout. Your attire should fit into the corporation where you are interviewing—whether you are already employed there or hope to be. Recognize that no matter how great your credentials, you cannot afford to neglect the very first messages you are communicating in face-to-face settings through your appearance and dress.

If you understand and accept that your appearance will actually affect others' perceptions of your competence—your actual technical skills and abilities—as well as their emotional response as to your likability, you are on your way to success. You can fight this concept and lose the battle (your goal) or use it to your advantage and win—win what you want from the situation. In this case perhaps another interview and eventually the job offer or a super performance appraisal. Your appearance and dress can give you the extra edge when you groom and clothe yourself to fit the situation. Sell yourself and your abilities with a professional image. The savvy interviewer enhances his competency to get hired, get promoted, and earn more money.

Good Grooming Pays: Men

Good grooming isn't just a good idea, it is essential to the competent image you want to convey. Little things are noticed and do make a difference. Dirt under one's fingernails or a badly frayed shirt collar on a man applying for an executive position can be knockout factors without his ever knowing it. What employer is going to tell the candidate these were reasons he was not selected!

You can't afford not to pay attention to details of grooming and selection of apparel. You are the package you are selling. The wrapping on the package suggests both the care that was taken putting it together as well as the value of what lies inside. No detail is too small to be of concern and no message too unimportant to hone.

Hair

Mid length hair is recommended. Hair should neither be so short it reminds one of boot camp nor long enough to look unkempt, shaggy or like the remnant of a protest movement. Have your hair trimmed at least every three weeks. Cleanliness is essential. Shampoo your hair every day. You may want to select a shampoo for dry hair—even if yours isn't—so as not to be too harsh with frequent use. Blow dry your hair. It will only take a few minutes each morning, but will give your hair a fuller, neater appearance. You may want to use a light spritz of a non-aerosol hairspray to hold—not glue—any wisps in place throughout the day.

Facial Hair

On most men, and in most business settings, elimination of facial hair is recommended. Generally, a beard or mustache calls attention to itself and interferes with the messages you want to communicate. If you decide to keep facial hair, make certain it is neatly trimmed and kept relatively short. If you have a heavy growth and an afternoon interview, try to shave again an hour or two before the interview.

Fingernails

Keep fingernails neatly trimmed with no sign of dirt under the nails—even if the job in question requires getting your hands dirty—and especially if it does not.

Body

It should go without saying that your body should be freshly showered—shower in the morning rather than the night before. Use a combination anti-perspirant deodorant. If you perspire you not only don't want it to smell; you don't want it to show! Make sure that any fragrance—aftershave or cologne—is lightly applied. You don't want to announce your entry with your aftershave.

Eyeglasses

Both the frames and lenses should be clean. The glasses frame should not be held together by tape or anything else other than the original hinges!

Shirt

This should be its first wearing since it was cleaned and pressed. Yes, pressed. If you are buying 100% cotton shirts, as you should be, your shirts will need to be pressed. No time to iron shirts? Your neighborhood drycleaner will launder and press your shirts for you. Even polyester/cotton blends that say "wash and wear" look better when they have been pressed. Once the collar or cuffs begin to fray, toss that shirt so you won't be tempted to wear it again. Avoid button-down collars on your dress shirts.

Suit

Your suit should be freshly pressed. It should be cleaned if needed, but many men have their suit cleaned when all it really needed was to be pressed. Over cleaning will shorten the life of your suits. If there are stains on it, by all means have it cleaned. If it is just a bit rumpled, send it for pressing instead.

Shoes

Shoes should be cleaned and polished. Soles and heels should be in good shape. If they look worn take them to a shoe repair shop or invest in a new pair.

Car

Car? Yes, your car. You never know when the boss will see you drive up or invite you to continue the interview over lunch with some other decision makers, and you are the designated driver! Wash your car, vacuum the inside and clean out those old candy bar wrappers from the floor. Take the baby's car seat out before you drive off for your interview.

Remember that you are "on stage" so to speak from the moment you drive into the company parking lot until you get back into your car and start home. Make sure everything about you conveys positive images!

Dress to Your Highest Potential: Men

Dressing to your potential conveys messages at two levels—the type of clothing to wear and the cost of that clothing and your accessories. For anyone reading this book, the type of clothing is clear. You must wear a dark business suit. The cost is also clear: buy the best quality you can afford. Higher quality will look better from the first day you own it and it will look good longer than an inexpensive suit. The same holds true for other items of apparel. In the end, we usually get what we pay for, and the more expensive item, if it looks better and looks better longer, may actually be a better value than the less expensive item.

You can shop discount outlets or sales in department stores if you have a discerning eye and take advantage of real value. But be careful not to be "taken in" by special purchase goods brought in by the merchant and made to look like a sale! If you can't spot the difference, take someone with you who can. Fit is extremely important. Few men can buy a suit off-the-rack that fits perfectly. Good tailoring services will be important to your look of competence. An advantage to shopping in quality stores is that their tailoring services are likely to be top-notch.

The advice that follows is directed toward the man who is interviewing for a professional job. A man interested in being hired and being promoted through the ranks of business or government will find the advice sound. However, a man who is interested in a career in the theater or as a model may find the following clothing advice too conservative for his audience.

Suits

Your suits will be both the most important and the most expensive item you will buy. Your suit should be a conservative cut, flattering to your build, fitted well—which will likely mean more than just hemming the trousers—and dark in color. The colors of your first two good quality suits should be a navy and a dark gray.

With these you can go through several interviews and look great. Navy and dark gray are the most powerful colors for business suits. Black, though darker and more powerful, is reserved for formal evening wear and funerals, and can actually be too powerful. You make the interviewer feel uncomfortable! Add to these two suits a navy blazer and a couple of pairs of medium to dark gray slacks and you have a professional look for those occasions when you don't want to clothe yourself with the power of a dark suit.

> You must wear a dark business suit. Navy and dark gray are the most powerful colors for business suits. Black, though darker and more powerful, is reserved for formal and evening wear and funerals, and can actually be too powerful.

Make certain the trousers are neither too short nor too long—though most mistakes are made on the side of being too short. The front of the pant cuff should be just touching the shoe. The trousers should neither be tight fitting nor baggy.

Wool is by far the preferred fabric for your business suits. Wool blends are fine if they retain the look of fine wool. Avoid silk, polyester, doubleknits or corduroy as fabrics for your business suits. Look for fine quality fabric and good tailoring. As you move up the executive ladder, the people who are making judgments about you have learned to discern quality of attire. If you want to fit in as one of them, shop for quality even as you carefully shop for price.

Dress Shirts

No matter what the fashion designers would have us believe, a white long-sleeved shirt still confers the most power on the wearer.

Solid white or a small, discreet, white on white pattern in a good quality shirt are best. A light blue is acceptable, and may even be preferable with the navy suit for men who should avoid the high level of contrast of white with navy as they put together their best and most powerful looks. (More on this in the next section.)

Make sure the collar size is neither too tight nor too loose fitting and that the sleeve length is right for you. The lower edge of the sleeve cuff should rest on your hands when your arms hang naturally at your side. Make certain that neither the collar not the cuffs are frayed. Dingy shirts and frayed fabrics should be the signal to jettison them from your wardrobe. A traditional barrel cuff is preferable to the French cuff. A French cuff is acceptable if worn with cufflinks that have a classic design and do not call a lot of attention to themselves. Make sure your cufflinks, if you wear them, are of the same metal color—yellow gold or silver —as your watch, rings, and belt buckle.

Dress shirts should be 100% cotton.

Shoes

Believe it or not, shoes may disappear if they are right for the rest of the attire, but they are one of the first things people notice if they are not appropriate. Your dress shoes should be visually light in weight. Leave boots and heavy shoes for casual wear or for sports. Even wingtips are not the perfect choice if they have thick rubber soles. Laced shoes are preferred, wingtips are great, but they should be (or look like) quality leather with a hard leather sole. Conservative slip-on shoes are acceptable but they make a different statement and do not convey the same power look created by a laced leather shoe.

The shoe color should be black or dark brown. Whether you select black or dark brown depends upon your suit color and your hair color. Hair color? Your hair color is a color you wear day in and day out. If your hair is black or dark brown—that color along with your trouser color can be considered when selecting your shoe color. However, if your hair color is blond, red or white, please don't try wearing your hair color as a business shoe color!

Socks

The socks that you wear with your business suit should be a dark, solid color (or have the appearance of a solid color), and should complement or match your suit color. Socks that match either your shoe color or your trouser color will be least obtrusive. Dress socks should be lightweight—no heavy sport socks please. The socks should be long enough that no bare leg shows when you are seated—even if your pant legs hike up a bit.

Neckties

A classic striped repp (repeat stripe) or a club pattern (a small conservative, classic emblem that is repeated to form an all-over pattern such as a mallard duck print) are always safe choices. Silk is the fabric of choice or a fabric that looks and feels like silk. The material should not be too flimsy—good interfacing should take care of this, but you want the knot to stay looking crisp.

Jewelry

Your dress watch should be visually light weight and thin, and look like yellow or white gold. No heavy, bulky sports watches or plastic watchbands please. A classic watch with face and hands is still the best choice. A wedding band (if applicable) and no more than one other ring worn on the other hand is all. That West Point class ring may be a "small talk" conversation starter! It goes without saying—no earrings or nose rings here. Try to keep your metal colors the same. If your watch and rings are yellow gold, select a belt with a gold buckle. If you have a tendency, when nervous, to fiddle with your ring—consider leaving all but your wedding band at home!

Eyeglasses

The shape of your glasses should be flattering to your face. If, for example, you want to make your face look more narrow, don't select glasses with lenses that have an elongated width. If you wish to deaccentuate a squarish shaped face, avoid a lens shape that is fairly square. Be aware of your skin and hair colors as you select the color of your glasses frames. If you have light skin and light colored hair, stay away from heavy dark frames. You want your glasses to complement your look, not stand out and call attention to the glasses. It is very flattering to select frames that closely match your hair color or skin tone.

Avoid dark tinted lenses. The eye contact you make with the interviewer is one of the tools you will use to project the image of your trustworthiness and sincerity. Eye contact will be one of the factors that will influence how well the interviewer likes you. You need clear lenses so your expressiveness will be conveyed. Remember too, that you already are wearing one set of frames for your eyes—your eyebrows. Select frames that are sized so the top of the frame is about even with the eyebrow. That way you don't end up with two sets of frames for your eyes!

Belts/Braces

A plain leather belt of the same dark color as your shoes or suit should complement your professional look. Your dress belt should not be too wide—about an inch to an inch and a quarter—with a conservative buckle. No large buckles with logos or turquoise stones please. Braces can be part of a professional look, but they are still a bit outside the mainstream. Unless you wear braces as part of your normal attire, select a conservative belt for the interview. Never wear braces and a belt at the same time.

Handkerchief

Your best handkerchief is a clean, white, pressed handkerchief carried in your inside jacket or pants pocket to use only if needed. Avoid a decorative handkerchief in your breast suit pocket. It can easily make you appear ostentatious or foppish. If you are over 60 and it's your personal style you can probably get away with it. But let judgment prevail. Remember, you do not want dress to be an issue. If in doubt, leave it out.

Wallet/Briefcase

Buy the best leather wallet and briefcase you can afford. They will not only look great, but they will last nearly forever! Select either black or dark brown. If either black or dark brown is your hair color that will be your best choice. The briefcase should be relatively slim. It should not look as if it is your flight carry-on for a week-end trip! Clean out your wallet and briefcase prior to your interview. Neither should be bulging with unnecessary items.

Pen

Don't ruin an otherwise professional look that exudes competence by carrying a cheap plastic pen with someone else's advertising logo on it. A nice silver or gold pen—try to match the other metal colors you are wearing—makes a positive statement. Or select a solid black, navy, or brown pen. It doesn't have to be a Cross metal pen or a Mont Blanc solid color pen, but one that looks like these will complement the image you have created. Carry your pen in your inside coat pocket—not your shirt pocket. Do not carry more than two pens together—unless you want to project the image of a nerd!

Notepad

If you carry a notepad, choose a white rather than a yellow pad and find a nice leather case to carry it in. It will look so much more professional than a naked yellow legal pad!

Overcoat/Umbrella

When the weather demands it, you will wear an outer coat over your suit coat and you may carry an umbrella. Select an overcoat—not a jacket—to wear over your business suit. Wool or a combination of wool/camel hair or wool/cashmere is best for a cold weather climate. Navy blue seems to be the predominate color found in the men's departments. It projects a professional image and looks good over either a navy or gray business suit. In warmer climates, a lighter weight trench coat with a zip-out lining may be the only dress coat you need. You may select a light colored stone or tan coat for your light weight dress coat. But do avoid the olive green-toned tan color that fills many men's departments these days. The olive green tint is not a flattering color on any man!

Your umbrella must be black with no designs or designer or hotel labels! A full size umbrella with the traditional curved handle projects an image of class far better than a collapsible umbrella. But even though these items should be chosen carefully, ideally your interviewer will never see them. In a later section, we will advise you to leave these things in a coat room if one is provided or otherwise in the reception area.

The culmination of attention to a lot a seemingly small details pulls together a look that exudes professionalism and competence. The nonverbal messages you convey, work for you and complement the verbal messages of the technical skills and experience you possess.

Your Extra Edge—Your Personal Coloring is Key: Men

The previous sections provided guidelines to men for gaining the maximum look of competence through nonverbal cues communicated through their appearance and dress. These messages actually increase the interviewer's perception of the interviewee's level of competence! However, there is one more consideration that can give you an extra edge—select your best shades of the colors that speak power and combine colors to complement your personal coloring and give you the greatest impact!

> Select your best shades of the colors that speak power and combine colors to complement your personal coloring and give you the greatest impact!

What difference do your best shades and how they are combined make? A man who has strong coloring can pair a pure white shirt with a navy blue suit and look both attractive and powerful which translates into a look of competence. However, a man with less strong coloring who pairs his navy suit with a pure white shirt can find that he not only looks less attractive, but also appears washed out—in fact he has diminished his power look! So you need to ask yourself:

- Can I wear navy and white together and retain my "power look" or does that much contrast actually diminish my look of power and competence?

- Can I wear a pure white or is a slightly cream toned white more flattering?

- Do I look better in a blued gray, a taupe gray, or a shade in between?

The answers to these questions vary with each individual and his own natural coloring. So it is important to know what the appropriate answers are for you. JoAnna Nicholson and Judy Lewis-Crum explain the four basic color types in their book ***Color Wonderful***. Let's find out where your coloring fits in terms of color type as classified by Color 1.

Identify Your Color Type: Men

- **Contrast Coloring:** If you are a contrast color type, you have a definite dark-light appearance. You have very dark brown or black hair and light to medium ivory or olive toned skin. Black men in this category will have clear light to dark skin tones and dark hair.

- **Light-Bright Coloring**: If you are this color type, you have golden tones in your skin and golden tones in your blond or light to medium brown hair. Most of you had blond or light brown hair as children. Black men in this category will have clear golden skin on their face and dark hair.

- **Muted Coloring**: If you are a muted color type, you have a definite brown-on-brown or red-on-brown appearance. Your skin tone is an ivory-beige, brown-beige, or golden-beige tone—that is, you have a beige skin with a golden-brown cast. Your hair could be red or light to dark brown with camel, bronze, or red highlights. Black men in this category will have golden or brown skin tones and dark hair.

- **Gentle Coloring**: If you are gentle color type, you have a soft, gentle looking appearance. Your skin tone is a light ivory or pink-beige tone and your hair is ash blond or ash brown. You probably had blond or ash brown hair as a child. Black men in this category will have pink tones in their skin and dark hair.

Some individuals may be combination of two color types. If your skin tone falls in one category and your hair in another, you are a combination color type. If you are uncertain as to which color type category you belong, you may wish to contact Color 1 Associates, Inc. by calling their toll free number: 1-800-523-8496. They can refer you to the Color 1 consultant nearest you.

Maximize Your Look of Competence: Men

If you have contrast or light-bright coloring you can wear a pure white shirt and pair it with a navy blue suit and look both powerful and great! If you are a contrast color type you may select fairly wide stripes in your repp tie and add to your great look. If you have light-bright coloring a smaller stripe (or other design) in your tie will be more enhancing. Both contrast and light-bright coloring are enhanced by a medium to high level of contrast, so further contrast in your tie will work to your advantage. Both contrast and light-bright coloring can also wear their white shirts with their gray suit and both look enhanced and retain their power look. Check several different shades of gray next to your face to determine whether a blued gray, taupe gray or a shade between is most flattering to your coloring. You can wear medium and dark grays, but some shades are going to work better on you than others. Take the time to compare different grays or if you feel you need help, consult a Color 1 professional. You will invest a lot of money in your wardrobe and the investment can repay you many times over if you make good choices.

If you have muted or gentle coloring you will find you look better in a less pure white than your contrast or light-bright counterparts. It may be hard to find a slightly toned down white shirt as the industry has not yet responded to this need. We are still talking white here—not ivory or beige. Your ideal white will still look like white, it is just not as bright or pure a white as much of what you will find on the store racks. Don't lose sleep over this, but if you have a choice between a shirt that is a bright, pure white and one that is a bit less bright a white, muted and gentle color types should select the less bright white shade. It will be more flattering and won't diminish your power look.

Muted and gentle color types really shouldn't wear their white shirt with a navy blue suit. That is too much contrast for your personal coloring; it actually diminishes your look of power! It weakens the statement of competence you want to make. Your most powerful combination will be your best shade of a medium to dark gray suit paired with your white shirt. Your second power look consists of your navy suit paired with a blue shirt.

A man with muted coloring can select a tie with a medium level of contrast or one that is quite blended and with a medium scaled pattern and look great. A man with gentle coloring also needs to select a medium level of contrast or a blended pattern, but will look most enhanced with a small design or pattern.

Whatever your personal coloring, you can enhance your attractiveness and maximize your look of competence by selecting your best shades of the power colors and combining them with the level of contrast that is right for you. This extra edge creates your greatest visual impact!

Good Grooming Pays: Women

Good grooming pays off and pays $$$. Your grooming pays off as an asset moving you toward your goal and grooming can actually add dollars to your paycheck—both as you negotiate a beginning salary at the employment interview and when dealing with one's promotion or pay for performance during the performance appraisal interview.

Hair that obviously needs a shampoo or broken fingernails with chipped polish give employers easy knockout issues without your ever knowing it. You can't afford to overlook details of grooming and selection of apparel. You are the package you are selling. The wrapping on the package suggests both the care that was taken putting it together as well as the value of what lies inside. No detail is too small and no message conveyed is unimportant. By your appearance, you will convey your awareness of the importance of a professional image, that you fit into the corporate culture, and that you are one of them.

The advice that follows is best followed by women who are pursuing a professional career—though not the oldest profession! A women interested in being hired and being promoted through the ranks of business or government will find the advice sound. However, a woman interested in a career in the theater or modeling may find much of the advice too conservative for her audience and her goal.

Hair

Select a style that is flattering to your face, a style that is current, a style that is simple enough and suited to your hair's "body" so you can keep it looking great every day. If you are over thirty-five, be careful that you are not still wearing your hair in a style that looked great a decade or two ago. Overly teased, bouffant styles can date you—even make you appear older than you are. On the other hand, if you are very young and believe that your youthful appearance is an impediment to being taken seriously in business settings, you may reconsider and change a hairstyle that looks like you belong at the beach on the set of Baywatch.

Your hairstyle should be appropriate to the texture of your hair. If your hair is coarse textured with a lot of natural body, you can wear hairstyles that women with fine, naturally limp hair cannot. Find a good hairstylist who can advise you on styles that are both flattering to your face and appropriate to the texture of your hair. Pay a little more, if necessary, to get this expertise. It is a worthwhile investment. Learn how to take care of your hair between visits to the hairdresser. Your goal is to keep your hair looking great every day—not just on the day of the interview. Always keep your hair squeaky clean.

> Your hairstyle should be appropriate to the texture of your hair. A good hairstylist can advise you on styles that are both flattering to your face and appropriate to the texture of your hair. Pay a little more, if necessary, to get this expertise.

The general rule of "Not Too Anything" applies. Hair should not be too long or too short, not too bouffant, not too red, black, blond or brown—in other words your hair color should look natural and be flattering to your skin's tone. This is not to say you should not color your hair—just that it should not look as if you color your hair. To keep your well-selected hair color looking natural, you must have any necessary color touch-ups done regularly—before it is needed. Like anything else about your appearance, your hair should not call attention to itself. If the interviewer is concentrating on your flaming red hair, the interviewer is not concentrating on your message. Anything about your appearance that attracts so much attention that people are talking about it after you leave, is almost certain to be a knockout to your candidacy.

Facial Hair

Make sure you don't have any facial hair. Check your chin in a mirror in good daylight and pluck any stray hairs. Make sure your brows are neatly shaped and pluck stray eyebrow hairs. The shape of your eyebrows can make you look tired, angry or older than your actual age. Check with the esthetician at your beauty salon to see if your brows are projecting the messages you wish to convey.

Fingernails

Again, you want to avoid "too anything". Your nails should not be too long, or too short, not too pointed or too blunt, not too brightly colored or too weirdly polished with purple, blue or other rainbow hues, nor decorated with small designs. Remember you want to fit in—not stand out!

Nails should appear naturally shaped which means a gently curved end. Avoid points that look like daggers—unless you are trying out for the lead in a horror movie—or very flat, blunt ends that look like shovels. A medium length (too short suggests you may bite them and too long and, you know, it's that horror movie audition again) buffed to a sheen or with a clear or very, very pale polish—no frosted shades please—applied is best. Make sure your nails are clean.

Make-up

Your goal is to look natural, yet enhanced. You should wear some make-up, but not too much. Too much make-up can make you appear older than you are or look as if you should be seeking a job in a different profession! However, don't go to the other extreme and wear no make-up at all. Every woman needs some make-up. It polishes and adds finish to your visual image and make-up is needed to balance the visual power of the business suit.

Select a foundation or make-up base that matches the skin tone on your neck. Why your neck? Because correctly applied, your make-up base will end where your neck begins. There should be no line; your face should blend seamlessly with your neck. Don't try to give yourself a tan by using a make-up base a few shades darker than the natural color of your neck. And don't let the salesperson sell you a base that has more pink tone in it than the skin on your neck. The natural red color in your cheeks is your blush color—not your skin color. Some women have pink tones in their skin color; others do not. Much of the make-up available is too pink for most women. If you wear a make-up base that is too pink for your skin, you will always appear made-up (not natural) no matter how little make-up you apply. You can't avoid it, because the line between your face and your neck will be evident and your face color won't look natural. Select your skin tone and apply the base lightly.

Your eye make-up should be limited to a lightly applied eyeliner and mascara. Just enough to highlight your eyes and make your enthusiasm more visible! No black mascara or eyeliner unless your hair color is black. Brown-black or brown will be more natural looking on lighter haired women. Blush, lightly applied, and lipstick will finish your look. Select blush and lipstick colors that don't overpower you. You don't want your lips to be the only thing the interviewer sees as you talk about your credentials!

Body

It should go without saying that your body should be freshly showered. Shower in the morning rather than the night before—you're
that much fresher! Use a combination anti-perspirant deodorant.
If you perspire—and who isn't likely to with an interview at hand—
you not only don't want to smell; you don't want it to show. Make
sure that your fragrance, if any, is lightly applied. Avoid heavy
scents, such as musk based fragrances. You don't want to announce
your entrance with your fragrance. Nor do you want it to be the
focus of the interviewer's attention! Again, the "Not Too" rule
applies—not too much fragrance.

Eyeglasses

Both the frames and lenses should be clean. The glasses frame
should not be held together by tape or anything other than the
original hinges!

Suit

Your suit should be freshly pressed. It should be cleaned if needed,
but it may only need to be pressed. Over cleaning will only shorten
the life of your suits, so if there are stains on it, by all means have
it cleaned. If it is just a bit in need of pressing, do that instead.

Blouse

This should be the first wearing for your blouse since it was
drycleaned or laundered. It should be wrinkle free and there should
be neither make-up traces on the neckline or the collar nor any
stains. There is really no such thing as wash and wear when it comes

to looking crisp. Make sure your clean blouse has also been pressed.

Shoes

Your shoes should be clean and polished if they are leather and freshly brushed if they are suede. The heels should be in good repair. If they look worn, take them to the shoe repair or invest in a new pair.

Stockings

There should be no runs or visible snags. You may wish to carry a second pair somewhere discreet—your handbag or your brief-case—in case you accidentally snag those you are wearing on the way to the interview.

Car

Car? Yes, your car. You never know when the boss will see you drive up or invite you to continue the interview over lunch with some other decision makers, and you are one of the designated drivers! Wash your car. Vacuum the inside and clean off the seats and the floor. Take the baby's car seat out before you drive off for your interview.

Remember that you are "onstage" from the moment you drive into the company parking lot until you get back into your car to drive home. Make sure everything about you conveys positive images!

> Remember that you are "onstage" from the moment you drive into the company parking lot until you get back into your car to drive home. Make sure everything about you conveys positive images!

Dress To Your Highest Potential: Women

Dressing to your potential conveys messages at two levels—the type of clothing to wear and the cost of that clothing and your accessories. For anyone reading this book, the type of clothing is clear. Your best choice is a business suit. You might get away with less, perhaps a conservatively tailored dress, but you are taking a risk that your candidacy will be taken less seriously. This is not the time or place to take risks. Dress to your highest potential means just that.

The cost is also clear: buy the best quality you can afford. Buy fewer, but better suits. Higher quality will look better from the first day you own it and it will look good longer than an inexpensive suit. The same holds true for other items of apparel and accessories. In the end, we usually get what we pay for, and the more expensive item, if it looks better from day one and lasts longer, may actually be a better value than the less expensive item.

You can shop discount outlets or sales in department stores if you have a discerning eye and can take advantage of real value. But be careful not to be "taken in" by special purchase goods brought in by the merchant and made to look like a sale! If you can't spot the difference, take someone with you who can. Because the person who is interviewing you very likely can tell quality from inferior goods. Fit is important. Men expect they will have to have tailoring done to the suits they buy, but women expect to be able to buy off the rack. Make certain every part of the suit fits well. An advantage to shopping in quality stores is that their tailoring services are likely to be top notch.

Suits

Your business suit will be both the most important and most expensive item you will buy. It is the single most important thing that will visually establish your credibility and hence your competence to the interviewer. Your business suit will project that you are a serious professional. True, other attire can be worn by professional women today—a well tailored, conservative dress or pantsuit is acceptable. Perhaps the second most powerful mode of dress for a professional woman is a base consisting of a tailored blouse and skirt of the same dark color worn with a blazer in a contrasting color or a plaid, in which one of the colors in the plaid repeats the color of the base. But none of these confer as much competence on the wearer or convey the same level of professionalism to the audience—in this case the interviewer—as the suit. The dress, base with a jacket, or pantsuit can be worn in most business settings, but they create less powerful and competent images than the business suit with matching skirt and jacket. Save the other outfits for occasions when you purposely want to convey less authority.

Your suit should be a conservative, classic style. Again, the "Not Too Anything" rule applies: not too short, not too long, not too fitted or nipped at the waist, not too bright. It should look like a business suit rather than a fashion or evening suit. You want to fit in—not stand out! A classic suit will serve you best for interviews and its classic styling will allow you to wear it for many years to come. The ideal fabric for your "look of competence" suit is wool or a wool blend. This will be easy to find in cool climates and during winter months—but much more difficult in the summer. It is still much harder for women than for men to find summer weight wool suits. Look for light weight fabrics that have the look of wool. Today, there may be some synthetics that fit this description. But be careful! The acceptable synthetic fabrics are likely to be found in more expensive ready to wear.

Dark, solid colors are your friend no matter what the season. Navy will be your strongest color for a suit. Other dark colors such as wine or gray will also convey competence. Be careful about black. A black suit can convey so much power it could be threatening to some interviewers. At the other end of the spectrum, black is a color associated with sexy images. So at best you walk a fine line with a black business suit. There are colors, such as red, that some women choose to wear to be noticed. Keep in mind that if the interviewer is noticing your red suit, it is a distraction from other messages you are communicating and it is an image that speaks less competence. Camel, beige, or light gray in summer may be tempting. But they do convey a different image. Studies show that women managers lose authority in summer when they are dressed in light pastel colors. Just remember the principles and make your choice.

Blouses

Your blouse should be tailored—not frilly with ruffles or lace. The lines should look good with your suit jacket and look good on you. Silk or a fabric that drapes and looks like silk are your best choices. The color should look good with your suit color and look good on you (see the next section) and not call undue attention to itself. A wine colored blouse paired with a navy suit can look wonderful as can a champagne colored blouse paired with navy. You really do have many choices available to you.

Shoes

Your shoes may be a smooth leather or suede—which is a bit more dressy and a bit more feminine. The pumps that will add the most to your credible image will be plain and unadorned or sport a very simple trim. Avoid little leather flowers or ornate bows on the pumps you wear with your business suits. A closed heel and toe is best, but a closed toe with a slingback shoe is a possible choice if your business suit has a visual lightweight look—most likely in summer months. Please no sandals with your suits. Strappy sandals just do not have the visual weight to complement a business suit. You are sending mixed messages and it looks like you just don't have your act together!

The best heel height is about 2 inches. The heel width should be what is in style without being on the "cutting edge". In general the "Not Too Anything" advice is good here: not too high, not too low (not a flat), heel not too thick, or too thin or too avant garde in shape. But the shape of the heel should be a current shape. Women's shoes a decade old, no matter if they have a 2 inch heel height will look dated. If a man interviews you he may not notice, but a woman will! Avoid boots and platform soles on shoes no matter how "in" they may be.

A dark shoe color with a dark business suit is your best choice. Your goal is an over-all polished, professional look of compe-tence. You don't want to call attention to your feet! Dark shoes that complement your business suit, such as navy shoes with a navy suit is a great look. If your hair is a dark color, your hair color is good basic shoe color to complement your business suits. Brown shoes with a wine colored suit look great. Your brown shoes pick up your brown hair color—a color you always wear!

Stockings

Your color choices for stockings include either your skin color or the color of your dark skirt or shoes. In other words, match your legs or bring the shoe color up or the skirt color down. This works best with stockings of a sheer navy tint with a navy suit and navy shoes. It can work with gray. We do not recommend wearing wine stockings even if they match both your skirt and shoe color. If in doubt, wear your skin color. Avoid selecting skin toned stockings that are too tan for your leg color or with too much pink tone.

It should go without saying that your stockings should be unadorned: no seams, no rhinestones or sequins, no butterflies!

Handbag/Briefcase

Select one or the other—a handbag or a briefcase. If you carry both a handbag and a briefcase chose a clutch that will fit inside the briefcase. Leather is your best choice and if your hair is dark try to select a handbag or briefcase color that will pick up your hair color. If your hair is brown, a brown handbag or briefcase will visually complement the brown hair color. The handbag color relates to a body color. Avoid selecting a black briefcase unless it is your hair color and if your hair is not black, avoid wearing black shoes unless you are wearing black as a predominate clothing color.

Jewelry

Keep the jewelry you wear to an interview understated and simple. The "Not Too Anything" advice is applicable: not too large, not too flashy, not too dangling, and not too many. A pair of simple gold or silver button earrings, no more than one ring per hand, a simple, thin dress watch—no sports watch, swatch watch or dripping with diamonds evening watch for the interview—and a tailored necklace or pin if it enhances the outfit is plenty. The metals should match one another. If your watch is yellow gold, the other metal colors should be yellow gold as well.

Accessories—Scarves/Belts

A small scarf at the neck, rather than a necklace, can complement an outfit and add a touch of color or even visually pull together the colors in a suit and blouse. A belt, if your outfit needs one, should be tailored and blend with or subtly enhance your attire without calling negative attention to itself. Large belt buckles with fancy designs, logos, or stones set in them are best saved for your casual or sporty looks.

Eyeglasses

The shape of your glasses should be flattering to your face. If, for example, you want to make your face look more narrow, don't select glasses with lenses that have an elongated width. If you wish to deaccentuate a squarish shaped face, avoid a lens shape that is fairly square. Be aware of your skin and hair colors as you select the color of your glasses frames. If you have light skin and light colored hair, stay away from heavy dark glasses frames. You want your glasses to complement your look, not stand out and call attention to the glasses. It is flattering to select frames that visually match your hair color or skin tone.

Avoid dark tinted lenses. The eye contact you make with the interviewer is one of the tools you will use to project the image of your trustworthiness and sincerity. Eye contact will be one of the factors that will influence how well the interviewer likes you. You need clear lenses so your expressiveness will be conveyed. Remember too, that you are already wearing one set of frames for your eyes—your eyebrows. Select frames that are sized so the top of the frame is about even with the eyebrow. That way you don't end up with two sets of frames for your eyes!

Pen

Don't ruin an otherwise professional look that exudes competence by carrying a cheap plastic pen with someone else's advertising logo on it. A nice silver or gold pen—try to match the other metal colors you are wearing—makes a positive statement. Or select a solid black, navy or brown pen. It doesn't have to be a Cross metal pen or a Mont Blanc solid color pen, but one that looks like either of these will complement the image you are creating.

Notepad

If you carry a notepad select white rather than a yellow pad and try to find a nice leather case or cover to carry it in. That will look so much more professional than a naked yellow pad!

Coat/Umbrella

When the weather demands it, you will wear an outer coat over your suit jacket and you may carry an umbrella. Select a full length coat rather than a jacket to wear over your business suit. A dark color will serve you best, but any neutral is acceptable. A dark coat, especially in the winter when your fabric of choice should be wool or a wool blend, has the added advantage of not shedding a light color onto your dark business suit. Avoid fashion colors such as purple or jade.

A dark neutral umbrella with no designs, or designer or hotel labels will be your best choice. If your umbrella matches the color of your coat, shoes or hair it will complement your look. Even though these items should be selected carefully, ideally your interviewer will never see them. In a later section, we will advise you to leave coats and umbrellas in a coat room if one a provided or otherwise in the reception area.

The culmination of attention to a lot of seemingly small details pulls together a look that exudes professionalism and competence. The nonverbal messages you convey, work for you and complement the verbal messages of the technical skills and experience you possess.

Your Extra Edge— Your Personal Coloring is Key: Women

The previous sections provided guidelines to women to gain the maximum look of competence through nonverbal cues communicated through their appearance and dress. These messages actually increase your level of competence as it is perceived by the interviewer! However, there is one more consideration that can give you an extra edge—select your best shades of the colors that speak power and combine colors to complement your personal coloring and give you the greatest impact!

What difference do your best shades and how they are combined make? A woman who has strong coloring can pair a pure white blouse with a navy blue suit and look both attractive and powerful which translates into a look of competence. However, a woman with less strong coloring who pairs her navy suit with a pure white blouse can find that she not only looks less attractive, but also appears washed out—in fact she has diminished her power look! So you need to ask yourself:

- Can I wear navy and white together and retain my "power look" or does that much contrast actually diminish my look of power and competence?

- Can I wear a pure white or is a slightly cream toned white more flattering?

- Do I look better in a blued gray, a taupe gray , or a shade in between?

The answers to these questions vary with each individual and her own natural coloring. So it is important to know what the appropriate answers are for you. JoAnna Nicholson and Judy Lewis-Crum explain the four basic color types in their book **Color Wonderful**, which is out of print and difficult to find. However, Joanna Nicholson's, **Dressing Smart in the New Millennium**, just recently off press, should be available in your bookstore or library. Let's find out where your coloring fits in terms of color type as classified by Color 1.

Identify Your Color Type: Women

- **Contrast Coloring:** If you are a contrast color type, you have a definite dark-light appearance. You have very dark brown or black hair and light to medium ivory or olive toned skin. Black women in this category will have clear light to dark skin tones and dark hair.

- **Light-Bright Coloring:** If you are this color type, you have golden tones in your skin and golden tones in your blond or light to medium brown hair. Most of you had blond or light brown hair as children. Black women in this category will have clear golden skin on their face and dark hair.

- **Muted Coloring:** If you are a muted color type, you have a definite brown-on-brown or red-on-brown appearance. Your skin tone is an ivory-beige, brown-beige, or golden-beige tone—that is, you have a beige skin with a golden-brown cast. Your hair could be red or light to dark brown with camel, bronze, or red highlights. Black women in this category will have golden or brown skin tones and dark hair.

- **Gentle Coloring:** If you are gentle color type, you have a soft, gentle looking appearance. Your skin tone is a light ivory or pink-beige tone and your hair is ash blond or ash brown. You probably had blond or ash brown hair as a child. Black women in this category will have pink tones in their skin and dark hair.

Some individuals may be combination of two color types. If your skin tone falls in one category and your hair in another, you are a combination color type. If you are uncertain as to which color type category you belong, you may wish to contact Color 1 Associates, Inc. by calling their toll free number: 1-800-523-8496. They can refer you to the Color 1 consultant nearest you.

Maximize Your Look of Competence: Women

If you have contrast or light-bright coloring you can wear a pure white blouse and pair it with a navy blue suit and look both powerful and great! If you are a contrast color type you may select a large print with fairly vivid colors in your blouse and add to your great look. If you have light-bright coloring you too can wear vivid colors, but a smaller print in your blouse or a scarf will be more enhancing. Both contrast and light-bright coloring are enhanced by a medium to high level of contrast, and can wear fairly clear colors and look enhanced as well as retain their power look. Solid colored blouses will

> Whatever your personal coloring, you can enhance your attractiveness and maximize your look of competence by selecting your best shades of the power colors and combining them with the level of contrast that is right for you.

work better for the interview than most prints. If you select a print avoid a floral print of any size. Floral prints shout "little girl' and will diminish your competent image.

If you have muted or gentle coloring you will find you look better in a less pure white than your contrast or light-bright counterparts. Your ideal white will still look like white on you, it is just not as bright or pure a white as much of what you will find on the store racks. Your shades of all colors will be less bright, more toned down, than those worn by women with contrast or light-bright coloring.

Muted and gentle color types really shouldn't pair a white blouse with a navy blue suit. That is too much contrast for your personal coloring. The powerful contrast of navy with white actually diminishes your attractiveness (washes you out) as well as diminishes your look of power! It weakens the statement of competence you want to make. Your most flattering and powerful color combinations will be more blended. Try pairing a champagne, rather than a white blouse with your navy suit. Or try a blue or wine colored blouse with navy. Of course, black and white together is too much contrast, but if your hair color is brown you should be able to get a high level of contrast by pairing your toned-down white color with brown. If you are unsure of your color type or wish to have a handy guide to all your best shades of all colors in the best clarity for you, contact a Color 1 Associate. It is an investment in your look and your future that can pay handsome dividends.

Whatever your personal coloring, you can enhance your attractiveness and maximize your look of competence by selecting your best shades of the power colors and combining them with the level of contrast that is right for you. This extra edge creates your greatest visual impact!

5

SPACE AND TIME: TWO-WAY MESSAGES

Our use of space and the elements that occupy that space conveys messages to those around us. If we can be attuned to receiving the nonverbal messages conveyed by those around us, and respond appropriately to those messages with our own behavior, we can interact in more positive ways with others. Those individuals who are viewed as insensitive to those around them are often individuals who do not pay attention to others' nonverbal cues. The savvy interviewee is alert to others' nonverbal behavior and is sensitive to the messages conveyed. He will respond to the interviewer's behavior in ways that will not create discomfort with the interviewer. He will try to fit into what he perceives to be the interviewer's expectations for the situation.

If you approach another individual too closely—thereby violating his bubble of personal space—he feels uncomfortable. If you sit in the wrong place, if you reach out and touch him when he does not want to be touched, he feels uncomfortable. If the interviewer feels uncomfortable three negative things happen. First, the interviewer begins to dislike you. We tend not to like people who make us feel uncomfortable. Second, the interviewer begins to believe you are not "one of them" because if you make him feel uncomfortable, you obviously do not fit into the organization's corporate culture. Third, much of your verbal message is now lost on this interviewer. The interviewer's concentration is focused as much on his feelings of discomfort as on the verbal message you are conveying.

Our respect for the other person's time also sends messages—that we understand they are busy people whose time is valuable. A person who arrives late for the start of his interview has made a mistake from which it will be very difficult to recover. If we arrive late, we have abused the other person's time and sent the message that our time is more important than theirs. In addition to being irritated, the interviewer may infer that the interviewee is not very responsible: that if hired, he will frequently be late for work and may be late in meeting project deadlines as well.

Any excuse you make for your tardiness, short of death, is likely to fall on deaf ears. After all, the boss has heard all the excuses already and has had his share of employees who always have a ready excuse for their tardiness. One more irresponsible employee is not what he needs!

Personal Space and Conversational Distance

Proxemics is the term used in nonverbal communication to denote the spatial separation between people. Whether we call it proxemics, personal space or appropriate social distance, we make other people either comfortable or ill at ease by how we make use of the space around us and them.

When entering an office where you are reporting for an interview, if you notice the receptionist behind a desk, you wouldn't dream of walking around the desk to stand behind her to talk to her. That desk sets boundaries that we understand—these boundaries are partially physical, but also psychological. A young child entering the office just might run around behind her since there is no actual physical barrier to prevent it. The child's parent would probably indicate to him that he shouldn't do this and over time we become socialized as we learn about the psychological barriers our society recognizes and enforces.

So you will approach the receptionist's desk and standing at least a few inches from it, you will indicate your name and the name of the person with whom you have an appointment. The receptionist will probably ask you to take a seat, and you know she is indicating you should sit down—not physically remove the chair to some other place! Treat her well. Employers often ask the receptionist her impressions of job candidates. If you are wearing an overcoat, boots or are carrying an umbrella, ask the reception ist where to put them. If there is no coatroom, ask if you may leave these things in the reception area. Do not wear an overcoat into the interview. The nonverbal (and perhaps subliminal) message you are sending is that you are only there temporarily. You do not belong there. You will be leaving soon.

As you sit in the reception area you may be observed by others. Everything you do is on stage. Select reading material that conveys positive messages about you, about your interest in business matters in general, and about your interest

> In the reception area, select reading material that conveys positive images about you, about your interest in business matters in general, and about your interest in the company where you are interviewing.

in the company where you are interviewing. Your first choice of reading material should be any corporate materials you find in the reception area. Any additional information you learn about the company should be a plus as you engage in the interview. If there is no company literature available, select a business magazine to read as you wait.

If the interviewer comes out to greet you, stand up to full height before you extend your hand to shake hers, look at the interviewer and smile as you indicate that you are pleased to meet her. Follow the interviewer back to her office, and wait for her to indicate where you should be seated. If the receptionist takes you to the office to meet the interviewer, stand while waiting for her to indicate where you should sit. The interviewer should stand to greet you. If she does, then smile and indicate you are pleased to meet her as you extend your hand to shake hers. Occasionally the interviewer will not rise to greet you but will remain seated. In this case smile and indicate you are pleased to meet her and wait for her to indicate where you should sit.

Don't ever touch or pick up something from the interviewer's desk unless asked to do so. If something on the desk really intrigues you—perhaps you even believe it indicates a common interest and will build rapport—ask if you may pick it up. We can't imagine the interviewer will say no, but your asking puts you in the category of a sensitive, well-mannered individual and should not make the interviewer feel uncomfortable. If you simply pick up the object, some interviewers may feel that you have been a bit forward and their level of discomfort may rise slightly.

Don't remain standing after being invited to sit. If you are showing something to the interviewer such as a portfolio of your work, do not get up and walk around behind the desk and stand over him. This is engaging in several behaviors guaranteed to raise the other person's discomfort level. You should neither stand over his head nor presume to walk behind the desk to stand next to him. If he has chosen to sit behind a desk, as we shall see in the next section, he has chosen to position himself behind a barrier. Don't cross it without being asked.

Take a cue from what we have noticed the wait staff in many restaurants doing lately. When they approach the diners' table they introduce themselves, and then bending at their knees, crouch so they are at eye level with the diners as they describe any special features for that evening. The waiters are no longer hovering above the diners' heads. The waiters in the restaurants that are doing this indicate that their tips are up! Keep yourself at eye level with the interviewer by remaining seated; you have more at stake than an evening's tips.

From the first moment you meet, the interviewer will be giving you cues—some verbal, others nonverbal—as to the level of formality he is comfortable with during the interview. If the messages you are receiving indicate that this interviewer conducts a formal interview, you must adapt your style to match his level of formality. Don't make the mistake of trying to relieve your nervousness by making several jokes in an attempt to break your tension. You will only increase his tension. He will feel you don't fit in; you don't take work seriously; you are not right for the job; you are not one of them. It doesn't matter that your credentials say you are a perfect fit for the job! You don't fit! He may even lament after you leave that you looked so promising on paper. "Too bad," the interviewer may say, "but he just wouldn't work out here."

If, on the other hand, the interviewer has an easygoing, relaxed manner try to fit your style to his. Remember, the interviewer is conveying nonverbal messages as to what makes him comfortable. You must respond with nonverbal messages that indicate, I understand and respect that; I will not make you uncomfortable; I am like you; I will fit in!

Seating Choices

The seating choices will most likely be made by the interviewer. From the way the office furniture is arranged to where he motions for you to sit, these elements are in the hands of the interviewer. From the furniture arrangement to the kinds of things that adorn his desk or the walls, there are messages there to be read and interpreted. Your goal is to adapt—be yourself, but from your range of styles adapt your style to fit that of the interviewer.

If you interview in an office the most likely seating arrangements will be:

- face-to face across a desk with the chairs on opposite sides of the desk

- the interviewer on one side of the desk with the chair for the interviewee placed at the side of the desk

- face-to-face seated on opposite sides of a coffee table

- corner to corner—seated with chairs at 90 degree angles, usually at corner sides of a coffee table

- side by side on a sofa

The desk and the coffee table both act as barriers. The coffee table, however, is less of a barrier than is a desk. And an extremely large desk not only says something about the interviewer's status at the company, it also acts as a greater psychological barrier than a smaller one. Interviewers who prefer a more formal interview style often opt to conduct the interview from their position of authority behind their desk. If an office has both a desk area and a seating area, many interviewers will ask the applicant to be seated on one side of the coffee table and then he will take a seat in a chair on the adjacent side of the coffee table. This option usually suggests the interviewer is comfortable enough with authority that he does not have to be seated behind his desk. It also suggests a less formal interview style and may indicate that he is purposely trying to put the candidate at ease. Sitting side-by-side on a sofa is too relaxed for most interviews and creates difficulty for the participants to establish good eye contact. It is awkward at best, and to many individuals it may feel too intimate for a job interview.

Recognizing these differences in seating arrangements may provide clues about the interviewer and the likely degree of formality to expect for the rest of the interview. It may also help you to understand why you feel uncomfortable in some situations. The degree of formality may be greater or less than you are used to or feel comfortable with.

If you are showing items in a portfolio to the interviewer, the corner to corner arrangement over a coffee table works well. You can establish eye contact easily and can both look at the work you have produced. If you find yourself across the desk from the interviewer and need to share your portfolio items, your best bet is to stay seated on the other side of the desk unless the interviewer suggests to you to do otherwise. Do your best to find the items you want him to note, and point to them from your upside down vantage point. You may want to practice doing this at home—just in case. Seated side-by-side on a sofa seems too intimate for most interview situations—almost as if you are looking over the family photograph album! If you find yourself in this seating arrangement, you may want to leave more space between you and the interviewer so you can sit forward a bit on the sofa and turn your seated body so you are nearly forming a 90 degree angle similar to what we discussed earlier. This creates space that should make you both feel more comfortable while affording you opportunities for better, and more comfortable, eye contact.

Conversational Space

Each one of us carries an area of space around us—a personal bubble—that we do not expect strangers to intrude upon. This space is invisible both to ourselves and to others, but it is very real. The amount of space necessary for us to feel comfortable varies with the norms of the culture from which we come and varies with individuals based on personal norms. We feel uncomfortable if a stranger sits too close to us on a park bench. We feel uncomfortable when we are crowded together on an elevator. In fact, we feel so uncomfortable on the crowded elevator that we will not even make eye contact with the other people. Every single person on that elevator—except for small children—will have eyes fixated on the floor numbers flashing by above the elevator doors!

If we violate another individual's personal space, we will make that person feel uncomfortable. There are general guidelines that indicate what spatial distances are comfortable for most individuals under various social settings. These guidelines apply to North America and are not the same worldwide. The intimate bubble ranges from actual physical contact to an outer limit of about 18-24 inches. Obviously there are some situations where individuals desire this close proximity with each other, however, an interview is not the appropriate situation. The personal bubble encompasses an area of about 18-24 inches at the closest to about 4 feet at the outer limit. This is appropriate for carrying on discussions that are intended

> An interview setting falls into the lower limits of the social bubble of conversational space. Most individuals will feel comfortable participating in an interview at distances of between 4-5 feet from the other individual.

to be private. The social bubble covers an area of 4-12 feet and is commonly used for casual exchanges where it is okay if others overhear. Distance of greater than 12 feet is normally used in formal situations—a public speaking setting would be an example of this.

Thus for most people, an interview setting falls into the lower limits of the social bubble. Most individuals will feel comfortable participating in an interview at distances of between 4-5 feet from the other individual.

Cultural Differences and Personal Space

The norms suggested in the previous section hold true for most North Americans and Northern Europeans. Other cultures, such as those in the Middle East, Latin America, as well as Southern

Europeans tend toward closer proximity. So if you are interviewing for an international job overseas, you may find you feel uncomfortable as the interviewer follows norms for social distance that are much closer than you are used to. Or if you are reading this book, and you grew up in one of the cultures mentioned as establishing closer proximity when engaged in conversation with others, you need to be alert to signs that you are making the interviewer feel uncomfortable by your closer proximity than the norms he is used to.

How do you know you are too close to the other person? If he keeps backing up from you, that is a pretty good indication that he feels uncomfortable and is trying to establish greater personal space. It is literally possible to back another person across a hallway and up against the wall on the other side without his ever consciously being aware what is happening. He just knows he feels uncomfortable. And again, you never want to make the interviewer feel uncomfortable!

Read the Interviewer's Cues—
Use Space to Your Advantage

Start by establishing social distance, except for the initial handshake, at about 4 or 5 feet apart. This should be a comfortable distance whether seated or standing, for both you and the interviewer. Take your cue from the interviewer as to where to sit. Be alert as to the degree of formality of the interviewer and try to follow his lead.

Make Time Your Ally

We each have only 24 hours in each day. We can't get anymore, so we have to make the most of those 24 hours we have. How you manage time says a lot about you, how you value other peoples' time and how dependable you are.

The adage that you never get a second chance to make a first impression makes it imperative that the first impression you make on the interviewer is a good one. Unfortunately, if you are late for your interview, those crucial first five minutes leave a lasting blemish on your candidacy. If you keep the interviewer waiting, you have conveyed that his time is not important to you. That you consider your time to be more valuable. That you are not a very responsible person. That you may be late with everything else. You will miss deadlines that can cost the company money.

You may believe you had a legitimate reason for being late, but what constitutes legitimate? You apologize and tell the interviewer that the traffic was really awful. Might a responsible person—especially one going for a interview—be on his best behavior and have made allowances for the possibility of traffic jams? Or you tell the interviewer you had a flat tire on your way to the interview. This does stretch credulity and is unlikely to even be believed, but again, an early start with extra time to get to the interview would have helped. Are you going to tell the interviewer that you got lost and couldn't find the right place? This will either indicate that you can't follow directions very well or that someone in the company did not give you good directions—either interpretation and you lose!

"But," you say, "I don't make a habit of this. This is the first time I have ever been late." But the interviewer doesn't know that! It is one time out of one for him. He has little other information to go on. The savvy interviewer recognizes he has no prior track record with this interviewer. The interviewer will respond based on this one situation. So put your very best foot forward, put it in the right place, and put it there on time!

6

MAKE YOUR BODY LANGUAGE
SPEAK SUPERLATIVES

You may recall that in the period between the time that the Iran Contra story broke and when the televised Congressional hearings involving Oliver North began, at the time when we had heard only the verbal accounts by others about the person Oliver North was, he was made out to be a "loose cannon" who had been out of control. That one term—loose cannon—seemed to sum up the impression most of America had of him. Then came the Senate hearings and much of the country watched on television as a composed, calm, in-control person epitomizing military bearing testified before Congress. Chances are most Americans can't recall what Oliver North said. Yet his demeanor changed the opinions much of America had of him. Even those who still did not like him or his views or actions felt less negative than they had prior to seeing the hearings.

Or recall that in the much discussed Nixon-Kennedy debates held prior to the 1960 presidential election, those who listened to the debate on the radio thought Richard Nixon had clearly won. But those who watched the televised debates concluded John F. Kennedy was the winner. The verbal elements were exactly the

77

same for both audiences. Clearly the nonverbal visual elements gave Kennedy the edge.

Your body language can enhance your credibility or it can rob you of your perceived competence. Make yours speak superlatives!

Nonverbal Behaviors That Regulate Interaction

A wave, a broad smile flashed across the hallway, an upturned head nod signifying recognition—these are all ways in which we signal a greeting using our body. As we draw closer, we may shake hands or share a greeting hug. We may signal that we are about to close our present interaction by looking at our watch in an obvious manner; placing our hands on our thighs, as if for leverage in getting up if we are seated; or by gathering together a set of items from our desk, such as the pages of the applicant's resume. As we actually take our leave we may engage in behaviors that signal we are terminating our present meeting, but the relationship is only coming to a temporary close as we smile, have a forward lean to our body, or perhaps shake hands with one another.

The give-and-take of our conversation with others is largely regulated by nonverbal behaviors through which we recognize that the other person is ready to yield to us or we indicate to our conversational partner that we are ready to yield the floor to him. We signal this readiness in part through our vocal inflection, but also through our body language. As an individual is ready to yield his speaking turn, his gestures are likely to slow or stop and the body tenseness, which was subtle but present, is likely to become more relaxed. When we wish to maintain our speaking role and not yield our turn, we will continue our gestures and body tenseness. When the other person continues talking beyond what we believe to be their appropriate turn, we may nonverbally request our turn by straightening our posture and leaning slightly forward in our chair or if standing, moving slightly forward into the conversation. We expect the other person to be responsive to our body language and give us a chance to speak.

Our behavior is constantly communicating messages to those around us. Slumped shoulders tend to be read by others as meaning that you have the weight of the world on your shoulders, have given up or are nearly beaten. If you have poor posture and tend to slouch, now would be a good time to start correcting this—before you get into the interview. Since messages that you are beaten down are not messages you want to convey. One or two fingers placed at one's lips tend to convey tentativeness or embarrassment. Closed fist gestures obviously convey aggression. Some people may have developed habits over the years that convey the wrong messages to others. Their friends have become used to the body language and no longer even notice the negative or unconventional behaviors. But the behaviors will be very apparent to people they are meeting for the first time.

> Slumped shoulders tend to be read by others as meaning that you have the weight of the world on your shoulders, have given up or are nearly beaten. If you have poor posture, start correcting this now—before you get into the interview.

Become sensitive to your body language and how it may be interpreted by others—especially those who are meeting you for the first time and don't know much about you.

Ask for feedback from others—ideally from people who can view you objectively as a potential interviewer might see you. If you conduct informational interviews, near the end of the interview when you are requesting feedback on your resume, ask your interviewee to give you feedback on the overall impression you convey to him. This person will be more similar to those who will be interviewing you later in your job interviews and since he does not know you well, these comments should be very valuable.

Once you have determined nonverbal behaviors you wish to modify, start by trying to change the behaviors in your daily activities. If you change your body language in your day-to-day routines, the new behaviors will carry into your interviews with you.

Communicate Positive Attitudes

How you stand and sit—what do you with your arms and legs, how you hold your head, your body orientation toward or away from the listener—communicate messages that are interpreted by other individuals as having positive or negative meanings. The listener (interviewer) may not even be consciously aware of what he is reacting to. But he knows that he feels comfortable or uncomfortable, likes or dislikes, trusts or does not trust, the other individual. If the interviewer responds negatively to the applicant's nonverbal communication, it will be difficult for the candidate to overcome those negatives no matter what the verbal interaction.

What then are the behaviors the savvy applicant should display? Behaviors that convey positive messages of both liking the other person and interest in the discussion are:

- body orientation toward the other person

- a slight forward body lean toward the other person

- openness of arms and body

- postural relaxation (but not too relaxed—not tense, but not slouched)

- direct eye gaze

- positive facial expression

Disinterest and/or dislike for the other person is conveyed when the interviewee leans back too comfortably in his chair, is slumped in the chair, constantly looks around the room, avoids eye contact with the interviewer, drums his fingers, wrings his hands, plays with his rings—perhaps turning them on his finger, fidgets, is stone faced or expressionless.

The applicant who slumps or leans completely back in his chair simply can't convey the same level of interest and enthusiasm from that physical position, no matter how wonderful the rest of his other nonverbal messages may be, as the person who sits straight up in the chair and with a slight forward lean. A slouching figure may be interpreted by the interviewer as a sign of disrespect as well as lack of interest.

Direct body orientation means that the applicant's body is facing the interviewer, rather than sideways to the interviewer. If you are seated directly across a desk from the interviewer this position will probably be automatic and natural. However if you are seated at the side of the desk with the interviewer directly behind it or in the corner to corner, 90 degree angle arrangement around a coffee table, you should position your upper torso to be facing the interviewer more directly. You can do this by sitting a bit sideways in the chair and further bending your upper torso, a bit if necessary, to face the interviewer.

Openness of arms and body means that your arms are at your side rather than folded across your body. If you fold your arms across your body, you may convey, perhaps on a subliminal level, that you are closed to the other person and to his ideas. The arms open position conveys that you are open and responsive to the other individual and to his message. Granted, there are other reasons you might fold your arms—simply being cold is one of them. But since closed body language might send a negative message, it is better to avoid the closed posture.

If you are too tense, you make the other person feel uncomfortable. There may also be a sense of wondering what it is you are trying to hide. So try to appear relaxed and comfortable—it will help the interviewer feel more comfortable—while at the same time not engaging in so much postural relaxation that you are slouching!

> The most important positive attitude you can convey is your enthusiasm—through your tone of voice and facial expression—as well as through your use of gestures and body language.

By far the most important positive attitude you can convey is your enthusiasm—often referred to as dynamism. By your dynamic attitude you convey your interest in the other person, in the company, and in the job as well as toward life in general. You convey your dynamism through your tone of voice and facial expression—both topics of future chapters—as well as through your use of gestures and body language. Of course gestures can be overdone, but that is far less frequently a problem than the individual who uses few, if any, gestures. Gesture occasionally, naturally, and appropriately to reinforce your message. Do avoid wild gestures that are all over the place and that detract from, rather than reinforce your message.

It is also a good idea to keep your hands away from your face. Both men and women can exhibit preening behaviors as they push hair back out of their face or perhaps unconsciously try to fix or rearrange their hair. Women may unconsciously play with an earring. Or an interviewee may nervously scratch his face or head or push back the cuticles on his fingers. These are distracting behaviors that will focus the interviewer's attention on the unwanted behavior rather than the applicant's positive verbal messages.

Try to avoid having a pen or notepad in your hands except when you are using it. Anything in your hands such as a pen or notepad becomes a likely thing for you to nervously play with. Either of these items in your hands will also impede your use of gestures. If you are holding pen and notepad in your hands, you are far less likely to gesture than if you are not holding onto them.

Avoid Communicating Messages of Deception

We learn from a very young age to engage in innocent deception. We receive a gift at our birthday party that we don't like, and what do we do? We are likely to make a sour face or outright tell the giver we don't like it. A parent is likely to tell us that this behavior isn't nice and direct us to apologize to our playmate. We are likely to hear more about our rude behavior after the guests have gone home! So we learn that some deception is okay. We feign appreciation for gifts that we really don't want and learn to hide our disappointment when we lose something we wanted very much. Have you ever wondered at the fact that the winner of the Miss America pageant is the only one of the contestants for whom it is socially acceptable to show tears? The losers must hide their own disappointment and show how happy they are for the young woman who did win the crown. Talk about putting on a happy face!

So we all learn, with varying degrees of skill and sophistication, to hide much of our true feeling. However, we may still communicate messages nonverbally that are counter to the messages we wish to convey. At times our verbal communication and our non-verbal messages may be contradictory. The listener may consciously pick up on these messages that are odds with one another, or may detect the inconsistency on a subliminal level. He may feel that something just doesn't feel right, but he can't put his finger on it. He is at a loss to explain what gives him the sense of unease.

However, there are behaviors individuals engage in that people do notice. These behaviors are seen as signs that the person is being less than completely honest. They are cues of deception. Individuals may exhibit some of these behaviors simply out of nervousness. But even if the interviewer recognizes them as being signs of nervousness, the question remains, why. Why is the applicant nervous? Is the applicant nervous because he has something to hide? Good grief, you may say, he's nervous because he is in a job interview and he has a lot at stake here. True, but the question and sense of unease remains nonetheless.

Your goal is to avoid raising any of these negative questions. So let's look at some of the cues that convey deception that you want to avoid. People who are lying tend to exhibit the following behaviors:

- less eye contact (fewer and shorter duration)
- use fewer gestures
- more shrugs of their hands
- less nodding
- slower speaking rate
- more nonfluencies
- higher pitched voice

Remember the saying often cited to indicate a person's perceived dishonesty—he couldn't look me in the eye. The individual who looks around the room, at the desk, the floor, or at his notepad too much of the time may be viewed as having something to hide from the interviewer. Aside from this interpretation of the motivation for the applicant's behavior, such conduct is likely to make the interviewer feel uncomfortable with all its ramifications.

The use of fewer gestures is seen as indicating less enthusiasm, and one is thought to be less dynamic when engaged in deceit. The liar is torn between reality and the deception he is trying to weave. The greater number of shrugs of one's hands results from their own uncertainty about the message they are communicating, and less head nodding results from the fact that the person is unconvinced himself and perhaps doesn't even agree, in reality, with what the other individual is saying. The slower speaking rate as well as the greater number of nonfluencies come about as the person has to think more carefully about what to say than he would have to if telling the truth. A voice that is higher pitched than usual, results from one's own unease and nervousness about the untruth.

Obviously many of the behaviors cited above can have other explanations—nervousness is an emotional state readily known to most anyone who has ever experienced a job or performance interview. And being nervous can cause many of these behaviors to appear. However, because these behaviors can also make the interviewer feel uncomfortable and may be perceived as negatives more serious than being attributed to nervousness, they are behaviors that one should avoid, or at least minimize their intensity and frequency.

We will look next at the positive behaviors you should practice in your everyday encounters with others. If you will engage in these behaviors in your day-to-day activities, you will find they will come more naturally to you in your interview encounters.

Put Your Best Foot Forward

Put your best foot forward and convey positive messages to others in your everyday life and in those important interviews you will encounter. From the moment you get out of your car in the parking lot until you are back in your car to drive home, consider that you are making an impression on someone. Do your best to make it a good one!

Walk with your shoulders back and your head held high. Your stride should be purposeful—not quite marching, but definitely a gait that conveys assurance. Your hands should be at your side. When you meet the interviewer extend your hand in a confident manner to shake his or hers. This should neither be a tentative, limp handshake nor a killer grip handshake. Extend your hand with your palm showing at a slight angle, grasp the other person's hand fully and firmly, web-to-web, shake once or twice and then let go. (The web is the area where the thumb and forefinger come together.) Your stance should be steady with both feet planted on the ground and your weight evenly distributed on both feet.

When seated, sit up straight with a slight forward lean and with your body oriented toward the interviewer. Keep your hands away from your face and don't play with your hair, your nose (which of course itches at this point!) or with a pen or anything else. Keep your feet flat on the floor—avoid crossing your legs or feet and by all means avoid drawing circles or making other nervous motions with your feet.

When seated, sit up straight with a slight forward lean and with your body oriented toward the interviewer. Keep your feet flat on the floor—avoid crossing your legs.

Synchronize Your Body Movements With the Interviewer's

Be alert to the messages conveyed by the interviewer and keep your behavior in synch with his. If he is enthusiastic about a point, your forward lean, intent gaze, and engaged expression can signal your interest as well. If the interviewer is relaxed and making chit-chat, you can lean back a bit and be comfortable as well. Be careful though, not to become too relaxed and be alert to cues that the interview has moved to another stage where a more engaged posture would be more appropriate. When the interviewer makes obvious moves indicating that the interview is nearing its close, you too should be moving in ways that indicate your recognition and assistance in reaching closure.

In an employment interview you are selling yourself—both your professional and personal skills and abilities. Your ability to fit into the organizational culture and work setting are every bit as important. The savvy interviewer prepares to be his very best self—both his verbal interaction and his nonverbal behaviors must consistently communicate his competence, value, and ability to fit in.

7

THE EYES HAVE IT: MAKE
FACIAL EXPRESSION WORK FOR YOU

Facial expression may be the most significant visual cue after one's appearance affecting how the other person will perceive you. The face is highly visible, and especially in the proximity of 4-5 feet—the distance at which most interviews take place—the face is where people focus most of their attention as they read the visual cues conveyed by the other person. In return, we try to convey facial responses appropriate to the individual and to the situation. We try to show that we are appropriately open and friendly to the other individual, yet with some reserve appropriate to the business situation.

Convey Appropriate Facial Expression

Of course you are neither going to be receiving nor sending facial cues in a vacuum. Much of what you respond to and much of what you convey by way of facial expression and eye gaze will be read as part of the larger aspect of body language. But both the face and the eyes are entities worth considering separate from the larger picture. As we interact within the proximity an interview affords, the face and eyes are major markers of messages we convey. By your facial expression and eye behavior you either add to your projected image as a confident and competent individual or detract from it.

It has been said that we are better prepared to deceive with our face than with any other nonverbal cue. We have learned to control facial expression better than we control our body language or our voices. We learn not to show our fear, disappointment or anger, or at least we are successful at showing appropriate and lesser amounts of emotions that might work against us as we interact with others. Certainly we want to be able to control these emotions in the interview. We don't want the interviewer to see how nervous we really are, for we rightly believe that will detract from the competent image we want to project. We want to convey our interest and enthusiasm.

The face and the eyes work together and should convey compatible messages. If the messages are not congruent it will be very disconcerting to the listener. So if you convey a smile with your face, send a congruent smile with your eyes!

> Throughout the interview, you want to change your facial expression as you listen and as you talk so that you are visually responsive to the interviewer's comments and add visual impact to your answers.

Certainly you should smile when you greet the interviewer at the start of the interview session. This smile should make you appear pleasant and truly glad to be there, but not a smile so broad as to be inappropriate to the business situation you are in. Throughout the interview, you want to change your facial expression as you listen and as you talk so that you are visually responsive to the interviewer's comments and you add visual impact to the answers and comments you give. Most of you will do this natu-rally. A few of you may find that you don't change facial expres-sion very much—you may sit impassively and listen to the inter-viewer frozen in one expression. If you sit stone faced throughout the interview, you cannot possibly convey to the interviewer that you are interested in him, in the company or in the job. No matter what you indicate verbally, the nonverbal message will cancel any verbal assurances of interest.

Again, you may want to enlist the aid of others. Try to get feed-back about your facial expression. Do you vary your expression as you listen to the remarks of others? Is your expression appro-priate to business settings? If people tell you that you are expres-sionless or that your facial expression consists of a stone face, start trying to get a greater variety of expressions into your face in everyday situations. You will carry that additional expression into the interview with you. Make what changes you can prior to your interviews. It will be one less pressure on you when you meet the interviewer.

This does not mean that you should sit through the entire inter-view with a broad smile on your face. Too much smiling can make you appear ingratiating or even weak. Women especially, must be careful to modulate their smiling behavior. Although individuals certainly vary, as a group, women tend to smile more than men. In fact, studies indicate that women engage in significantly more over-all facial expression than do men. This can work for or against them in the interview. To the extent that a woman engages in ap-propriate facial expression for the business setting, looking alert and interested in the comments of the interviewer and varying her facial responses to the listening and speaking roles and the various messages throughout the interview, this can make her seem interested and interesting as well as likable. Certainly this will serve her well over the candidate who sits through the interview with a frozen expression on his face—no matter what that expression might be. However, some women must guard against smiling too much. A woman who smiles too much will find she is not taken as seriously in business settings as she would like to be. Certainly men do not want to smile more than is appropriate for the situation either. But as a rule and as a group, it is women who must especially watch this—both because they are the ones most apt to smile too much, and it is more likely to be interpreted as making them weak.

Whether male or female, one of your goals is to appear pleasant, and an occasional smile can help you convey that you are a pleasant person, you would be a pleasure to work with and that you are truly glad to be there and meeting with this interviewer. Your face should convey a variety of expressions as you listen to and speak with the interviewer. As you listen to the interviewer, try to convey by your expression that you are truly interested in his insights. You should be. You should be alert to information that hints at where you do fit or will fit into this company. Are you likely to be offered the job? If this is a performance interview, does it sound as if you are likely to progress much further with this organization? In either case, do you want to work or continue to work here? It shouldn't be hard to appear interested, for there is much to be interested in. It is your work future at stake here.

Positive Eye Contact

"Look at me when I'm talking to you." Is there a person alive who hasn't heard a parent or a teacher say this to them at one time or another? Why? Because to make eye contact meant you were paying attention. Eye contact meant you were showing respect. To maintain eye contact with another conveys to them that we think what they are saying is important and we regard them highly enough to give them our full attention.

In some cultures, downcast eyes are a sign of respect. But in the U.S. business world, lowered eyes are a sign of passive behavior, which is analogous to weakness. It may even be viewed as a sign of disrespect! Lowered eyes definitely convey a lack of confidence and hence competence to most business interviewers in our culture. Meet the eyes of the interviewer confidently and do it often!

When we make eye contact with the interviewer:

- we seek feedback
- we signal we have completed our thought, and the other person may talk
- we express ourselves

We convey to the listener:

- we are confident and competent
- we are engaged in the discussion
- we like the interviewer
- we are one of you, we belong here

If the applicant exhibits a lack of appropriate eye contact, he will be assumed to be detached or disinterested or even odd! When studies were conducted to determine what elements of a speaker's behavior conveyed sincerity, eye contact was a significant variable. Those speakers who were rated sincere, looked at listeners an average of 3 times longer than the speakers who were rated insincere. Perhaps this gives true meaning to the perceptions that "shifty eyes" belong to insincere people or that if someone "can't look us in the eye" they are being devious.

Eye contact must be appropriate to the business situation. It should not be perceived as flirtatious, but as sincere interest in the content of the communication and the person involved. Too long a gaze can be viewed as indicating attraction to the individual that goes beyond the employer-employee relationship. Or too long a gaze, if combined with other congruent body language, can actually be threatening and an indication of anger as is indicated by the common phrase "he tried to stare him down." If the gaze is too long it can make the other person feel uncomfortable—threatened by either an inappropriate sexual connotation or by the threat of bodily harm. It is never to our advantage to make the interviewer feel uncomfortable.

> Establish enough eye contact with the interviewer to indicate an interest in him and the organization he represents. Demonstrate that we can interact appropriately with him and hence with others in a business setting.

So we want to establish enough eye contact with the interviewer to indicate an interest in him and the organization he represents. We want to convey that we like him as a person—as a business person. We need to demonstrate that we can interact appropriately with him and hence with others—co-workers and clients—in a business setting. You want to convey that you are an active and enthusiastic individual who can get things done. You are competent. The most positive eyes sparkle with a life that conveys this interest and dynamism. To be interested in the other person and the discussion pays him a compliment, makes him comfortable, and says, "I fit in." Of course, the sparkle in the eyes is best complemented by an appropriate smile on the applicant's face.

Your Face And Eyes Convey Powerful Messages

Ask any public speaker which listeners in the audience he will focus on as he delivers his speech. He will tell you it makes him feel most comfortable to focus on the folks with friendly faces; those who appear interested in him and his message. He will try to focus his gaze on a lot of the people in the room, but his eyes will come back again and again to focus on the friendly, interested faces in the audience. They give him a needed psychological lift; they make him feel good about himself. Is it any wonder he avoids the negative or expressionless faces and focuses on the positive ones? The audience member who sits at the edge of the chair, smiles and nods her head in agreement often, and exhibits a variety of positive and pleasant expressions on her face conveys that she is attentive to and interested in the speaker and his message.

Studies involving teachers in classroom settings find that teachers tend to "teach to" the students who appear attentive and interested. They too, naturally tend to focus their attention on the faces that give them so much positive feedback! They actually have to train and force themselves to pay greater attention to the others in the classroom—those with less facial expression or less positive facial expression.

You can convey messages of interest and enthusiasm. Smile appropriately; nod your head when you agree with what the interviewer says; maintain a look of interest and a variety of facial expression; keep your shoulders back and your head straight; establish eye contact with the interviewer enough of the time to indicate interest but not so much as to make him uncomfortable. These are behaviors good listeners have learned to engage in. Assess which behaviors, if any, you need to further develop. Work on any that you wish to improve, and you can convey marvelous messages of interest and enthusiasm that will translate to a perception on the part of the interviewer that you are a confident and competent individual.

8

YOUR WINNING VOCAL ADVANTAGE

Would Marilyn Monroe's image be different if her voice hadn't had that breathy quality? Would James Earl Jones' jobs as an actor or a spokesperson be as numerous if he didn't have that resonant voice? Would Jesse Ventura have been as dominant a boxer or politician if he had a small, squeaky, high pitched voice? Paralanguage, which includes our vocal projection, vocal variety, the timing and rate of our speaking, affects the image others have of us.

We can use our voices to move us toward our goals or we can allow our voices to hold us back. Whatever we do, whether or not our vocal attributes are congruent with the other messages we convey, our voice will contribute to the overall image others have of us when they encounter us in person. Our voice is even more significant to the images others form when they meet us via the telephone since they have no visual cues to assist them as they form impressions. Savvy interviewers use their voices to project images of confidence and competence.

Project Your Voice: Project Your Competence

You simply must project your voice if you want to be perceived at your most credible. Although projection is not quite the same as loudness of volume, most people use the terms interchangeably. Certainly you want to project your voice so that the listener (interviewer) can easily hear you, for one of the surest ways to distract your listener is to make him have to work to hear you. But just as important is what a lack of vocal projection does to the listener's view of the speaker's credibility. Low volume is perceived as a sign of weakness. Put more projection behind your voice and you will be judged as being more influential. Call it influence, power, authority, or credibility, your vocal projection is equated with your level of competence.

> Low volume is perceived as a sign of weakness. Put more projection behind your voice and you will be judged as being more influential. Your vocal projection is equated with your level of competence.

If you mumble, swallow your words in your throat, or just talk softly, you damage the level of competence you are viewed as possessing. Although men are certainly not immune to the problem, and should be sure to project their voices as they speak, women are more likely than men to speak softly. Perhaps this is because they have been taught that a soft voice was a sign of femininity and they have consciously tried to speak softly. Or perhaps they were taught as youngsters that children were to be seen and not heard. Whatever the cause, lack of projection will consistently work against anyone—male or female—in the business world. A feeble voice will make the speaker seem weak or even old.

To project your voice doesn't mean you have to yell. That's why we prefer to call it projection rather than loudness, although good projection does mean that you will be easier to hear. Granted volume does enter in, but projection comes in part from supporting the voice with breathing from the diaphragm.

Any of you that have ever played a wind instrument or taken voice lessons know about your diaphragm. But for those of you who do not, try the following in order to locate your diaphragm. Make a fist with your hand and almost as if you are going to do a Heimlich maneuver on yourself, place this fist at your midriff— just slightly pressing against your body. Then try to use the muscle in that area to physically push your hand outward. Once you have been able to push your hand, you will have found your diaphragm. Support your voice as you speak with breathing that uses this muscle.

If you know you speak softly—perhaps you have received feedback that indicates this—you will probably have to start your road to increased vocal projection by speaking in a louder tone than what sounds right to you initially. Look at it this way: whatever projection you normally use seems comfortable to you. However, you know—perhaps from what others have indicated to you— that your voice doesn't project well. If you continue speaking in the volume that is comfortable for you, you will continue to under project. So at first you will need to speak more loudly than normal. Again seek feedback from others, who will let you know if you have really overdone it, but we find this rarely happens! It is far more likely you will continue to project less than what is good for your advancement. Work on increasing your projection and volume in your everyday encounters. Eventually your increased projection will feel normal to you and you will carry it into your interviews without even having to think about it.

Man or woman, you can improve your projection and increase your volume. Females can use their voices just as effectively as can men. So, if you are a woman, don't fall into the trap of making excuses that because you have a female voice you can't project as well as a male. That kind of thinking is erroneous and if you decide to believe it, believe us, it will keep you from projecting as much credibility as you could otherwise. A strong, projected voice will serve you well as you convey to others your image of competence.

Pitch Patterns Speak For You

The opposite of a person who speaks with a variety of vocal inflections is someone who speaks in a monotone. Certainly you have heard people who speak in a monotone—there is little variety of pitch in their voice. What was your reaction? Was your interest in what the person was saying sustained for very long? Did you go away believing that this individual was enthusiastic about and really believed in what he was talking about? Pitch patterns or vocal variety serve several purposes which will be important to you in all your communication endeavors—not just in the interview setting. First, good vocal variety helps keep your listener's (or listeners') attention focused on your message. Your variety of vocal inflection makes listening to your message easier for your listener and results in better attention and better understanding. Second, good vocal variety enables you to convey to your listener your conviction about what you are saying through the enthusiasm you demonstrate. You sound as if you really mean what you are saying; you believe in it! Third, the increased dynamism which vocal variety gives to your speaking actually enhances your credibility. You also appear to know what you are talking about; vocal variety enhances your expertise! No interviewee can afford to lose the positive messages good variety of vocal inflection speaks for them.

A rising pitch on the last word of a sentence (or thought) signifies you are asking a question. A falling pitch suggests a suspicious or hostile attitude. Pitch pattern can also negate what we are saying verbally. You can verbalize "yes" or "sure" with a pitch pattern that indicates "no". Make sure your pitch patterns are congruent with the messages you intend to convey.

You will find that your facial expression impacts on your degree and kind of vocal variety. People with little facial expression are often also those who inject little vocal variety into their verbal message. The converse is also true. Individuals who have animated facial expression tend to have animation in their voices as well. Animation cannot be present in the absence of vocal variety! So if you determine that you want to improve your vocal variety, one aid will be to try to be more facially expressive. Again, work on improving your variety of vocal inflection in your day to day conversations, and the increased variety will go with you into your interviews.

Remember that when you speak with another person using the telephone, your vocal messages are the only nonverbal cues he has to form impressions of you and your competence. Many individuals therefore, are less dynamic when communicating on the telephone than in person. If an employer calls you for a screening interview, you can't afford to let the only nonverbal cues your listener will have, present anything less than your best self. So get feedback on your telephone demeanor and work to improve it if necessary.

A savvy interviewee simply must project his enthusiasm for himself, his accomplishments, and his goals through the use of a variety of vocal inflections.

Convey Your Competence With a Controlled, Confident Pace

Do you have a tendency to speak at one pace? When you feel nervous do you speak more rapidly than usual? Or do you speak so slowly that people want to finish your sentences for you? Your pace is the rate—how rapidly or slowly—at which you articulate words.

Ideally your speaking rate should be a comfortable one for your listener. Speak too fast and it is difficult for your listener to remain focused on your message. It is hard work to keep up with a person whose pace is too rapid, and after listening for awhile the interviewer may take a "mental exit". Speak too slowly and you will aggravate the interviewer.

Your speaking pace or rate says a lot about you. If you speak too fast you may sound like the stereotypical used car salesperson—like someone who is trying to pull a fast one (no pun intended) on the listener. A too rapid speaking rate may emphasize to the listener you are nervous or anxious. Speakers who are being deceptive tend to speak rapidly. A too rapid pace comes across as being "canned" or too practiced rather than being sincere. The rapid pace is also a distraction and the interviewer finds it difficult to focus on the message; instead he is focusing on the delivery itself. A person who consistently speaks too rapidly loses the listener, and loses some of his credibility.

Strive for a comfortable pace for your listener—the interviewer. Vary your pace. You can slow a bit to emphasize a point, and then pick back up to that comfortable listening rate. Varying your pace will help the interviewer keep focused on your message. A pace that is neither too slow nor too fast will build your credibility. A too rapid pace makes the applicant sound frightened; but a pace that is comfortable to listen to conveys that the applicant is confident of his messages.

Don't Let Nonfluencies Weaken Your Credibility

Silent pauses can strengthen your message. Vocalized pauses will weaken your message and weaken your credibility. A vocalized pause or a filler is a nonfluency; it is the space the speaker fills with words that don't belong to the message. Space filled with, "ah" or "and ah" is space filled with a vocalized pause. Space filled with words such as "like" or "you know" is space with fillers. An occasional vocalized pause is not a problem. In fact, though we never encourage anyone to use vocalized pauses purposely, an occasional "ah" may convey that the applicant is thinking of his response as he speaks rather than having planned it.

> Vocalized pauses will weaken your message and your credibility. Once the interviewer focuses on the vocalized pauses, he begins to lose sight of the message.

Nonfluencies become a problem when done with such frequency that they call attention to themselves. They become a distraction. Once the interviewer becomes focused on the vocalized pauses, he begins to lose sight of the message. The outcome for the applicant is both diminished credibility, because he has seemed unsure of himself, and a diminished message, because the employer has been distracted and lost sight of the message. What has been communicated most forcefully are the nonfluencies.

If you sprinkle your speech with too many nonfluencies you probably already know it. But you can request feedback on this or carry a tape recorder around for a few hours and tape your conversations with friends. As with other habits you engage in, nonfluencies don't just suddenly appear in your interviews. The good news is that you can learn to limit your use of fillers and vocalized pauses. If you need to work on this, try the behavioral modification steps that follow. These steps do work. We have seen people significantly lessen their use of fillers and vocalized pauses in a relatively short time. You can also work on diction or other behaviors using this method.

1. **You identify a behavior you wish to change.** In this case you want to decrease your use of vocalized pauses.

2. **You make a commitment to yourself to change the behavior.** If you are really committed to the change, this process will work for you. But **you** have to want to make the change. Just the fact that someone else wants you to change is not enough.

3. **You must become aware that you have engaged in the behavior** each time you have done it. This happens after the fact, but nevertheless you must be aware that you have "done it again". You may wish to enlist the aid of another person(s) to let you know you have done it—perhaps a friend at the office and your spouse at home. This person should gently remind you that you have just said "ah" again—or whatever the thing is you are doing and wish to change.

4. As time goes by, **you will become aware of what you are saying as you are doing it.** Because you are in the midst of saying it, you will not be able to modify it at this point, but your awareness of the behavior is coming about earlier in your speaking.

5. As more time goes by, **you will be aware you are about to say the thing you want to change.** At this point, with the earlier awareness, you can modify what you are about to do. For example, in this instance, pause with silence rather than filling the pause with sound.

6. With more time, **the new behavior will have replaced the old** and will come as naturally to you as the initial behavior did at one time. You will no longer have to think about what you are doing. It will now be your normal behavior—both as you converse with friends as well as in an interview situation.

Several of the above steps have indicated "as time goes by" or "with more time". The actual time needed to make a new behavior yours, varies with the individual and with his dedication to the process. We have seen this method work wonders in as little time as one week. The good news is that the behaviors that are modified in your daily interaction will carry over into other settings as well, whether it be an important interview or to give a public address!

Make use of silent pauses to emphasize thoughts, provide an opportunity for your listener as well as you to have a moment's respite, and to provide variety to your conversational speaking pace. Pauses break information into meaningful segments that make it easier for the listener to comprehend. Pauses give you a moment to reflect on your response. But avoid filling those positive silent pauses with vocalized sounds that say nothing other than that you are nervous, or hesitant, or unsure of what you want to convey. An abundance of vocalized pauses will weaken your credibility and lower the employer's perceptions of your competence.

Avoid Poor Diction—A Credibility Robber

Strive for clear diction and correct pronunciation of every word you utter. With clear diction and proper pronunciation, your message will be easily understood by the interviewer. What's more you will convey that you can interact with their clients, that you will fit into the organization. You make the interviewer feel comfortable because you are one of them! You will be perceived as credible and competent.

Diction is the production of sounds. Diction may be slovenly and lazy or crisp and professional. Sloppy diction is exhibited when someone drops the "ing" sounds at the ends of words such as saying "goin" rather than "going" or when one doesn't clearly articulate such as saying "Adlanta" rather than "Atlanta". Sloppy diction creates the impression with the interviewer that the applicant is of lower education level, social standing, and position and hence lowers his credibility and competence level in the perceptions of the employer.

Pronunciation is how you deliver words—where the accent falls as well as the actual pronunciation of sounds. Some elements of pronunciation vary with geographical region. In parts of New England, "idea" becomes "idear"—in fact all words ending in "a" are given the "ar" sound. "Car" becomes "cah", sounding more like the sound of a crow than a vehicle to drive. Know that when you interview within your own region where this is the acceptable pronunciation these regionalisms will not work to your disadvantage. In fact they may be a plus—you are one of them! However, if you are engaged in a nationwide search and you interview outside your geographical region, you may exhibit speech patterns that are distracting to the interviewer. These idiosyncrasies could even diminish your perceived level of credibility and competence. Now you are not one of them!

The importance of correct pronunciation would suggest that you be certain of the pronunciation of the names of the individuals you will be meeting, and try to anticipate any industry or geographic specific language you can anticipate using during the interview. The wrong pronunciation will make you appear less knowledgeable and well informed, and at worst, may actually offend your interviewers.

Make a habit of using clear diction and correct pronunciation in your day-to-day conversations and you will carry it automatically into your interviews.

Put Them All Together and You're Dynamic

If you will project your voice in a confident manner as you speak; vary your vocal pitch but strive for an enthusiastic manner of speech; deliver your message with a pace that is comfortable for your listener, but vary it a bit as well; pause, but make pauses silent space; avoid sloppy speech—pronouncing words clearly and correctly and you have the recipe for an individual who is demonstrating his enthusiasm while conveying sincerity. Your dynamic delivery will translate to the interviewer as confidence and be perceived as competence! It is yet one more aspect of nonverbal delivery the savvy interviewee uses to his advantage.

9

Don't Be Afraid of Silence

S ome people feel uncomfortable with silence—especially when we are with people we do not know very well. This is exactly the situation you find yourself in at many interviews. It is almost certain to be true at a job interview, less likely to be true at the performance appraisal. If you are afraid of silence, you are likely to rush to fill the void with verbiage. This could be your undoing. If you can become comfortable with silence, or at least mentally accept that it is okay, it will work to your advantage.

Don't Jump In Too Soon or Talk Too Much

The interviewer asks you a question. Though you do not want to pause for so long a time the interviewer becomes uncomfortable or thinks you have entered a catatonic state, feel free to take a few moments to consider your response. Be careful that you don't jump in too soon with your response. A moment's pause to compose your thoughts will work to your advantage.

Be careful not to talk too much. Some applicants talk on and on because they are afraid of silence. In a common scenario the candidate finishes his thought and pauses waiting for the interviewer to assume the lead, but the interviewer says nothing. The applicant begins to feel uncomfortable after a minute or two, so he decides he had better say something more. The "something more" may tell the interviewer far more than the well composed comments the candidate offered initially. The interviewer may simply be formulating his next comment or question, but he may be purposely confronting you with silence. First, he may want to see how well you handle yourself under the pressure to keep the flow of the interview going by speaking. Resist that pressure. Second, he may wish to see whether you will modify or retract what you have said. Maybe you will provide more information that will help him eliminate you from consideration for the job. A good interviewer will leave silence at the end of your answer. If you ramble on incoherently in order to fill silence, you will be rising to his bait.

> A good interviewer will leave silence at the end of your answer. If you ramble on incoherently in order to fill silence, you will be rising to his bait.

Of course silence can be uncomfortable. But when you are confronted with silence at the end of your answer, resist the temptation to talk too much. Fools may jump in, but you shouldn't! If the silence drags on for too long a time, you have three options which can reflect positively on you. First, you could ask the interviewer whether you have answered his question. This puts the ball back in his court and at least you should get a sense of what you should do next. If he asks you to clarify something, then of course do so—taking a moment first to compose your thoughts again. You may need to ask him to clarify what additional information he is requesting. Don't be afraid to ask questions that will give you a sense of the focus the interviewer is interested in hearing. Of course, if the interviewer was just trying to see how you would handle the uncomfortable silence, you have conveyed your ability to remain composed and handle the situation in a positive manner.

A second option is to suggest another question the interviewer might be interested in hearing about, "Perhaps you'd like to hear about..." The question you suggest should relate in some way to the question you have just answered and be one of your strengths that you would like to have an opportunity to talk about. Third, you could take the opportunity to ask the interviewer a question. Ideally the question you ask should be related to the areas you have been discussing. And do not ask self-centered questions at this point: no question about salary or benefits please!

Focused Silence in Salary Negotiations
Can Add $$$

If you can train yourself to be comfortable with silence, you may be adding dollars to the salary the employer was initially planning to offer you. When the employer indicates the dollar amount of the starting salary in the job interview, or the raise you are being offered in your performance review your natural inclination is to respond. Whether that inclination is to respond by accepting — whether eagerly or not the amount offered or whether your inclination is to try to negotiate a higher amount, don't jump in too fast. Be silent. Wait. You may be surprised how often the employer will feel uncomfortable with the silence at this point and jump in with a higher figure—without your having to say anything! And believe it or not, if you still remain silent, the employer may raise the figure yet again!

After the employer has increased your salary as a result of nothing but your silence, you still have the option of using whatever supports you have gathered for negotiating a higher salary, but at this point your starting figure may be several thousand dollars higher before you even begin negotiating!

Selected points of silence can work for you. If you find it impossible to sit there and say nothing as you look into the eyes of the employer, try taking out your note pad and pen and begin jotting numbers down on the notepad. This will give you something to do that will help you feel less uneasy and may further disarm the employer who assumes you are not satisfied with his offer and are working with figures that are an increase in the salary.

For further information on strategies—both verbal and nonverbal—for negotiating the best possible salary in the job interview see our book entitled, **Dynamite Salary Negotiations**. Readers who are preparing for their performance review may wish to get another one of our books entitled, **Get a Raise in 7 Days**.

If you recognize how you can make use of silence in positive ways, from the silent rather than vocalized pause, in the moments after you have answered a question when the interviewer says nothing, to your silence after the employer indicates the amount of salary or salary increase he is offering, you will have become a more savvy interviewee.

10

PUT IT ALL TOGETHER:
YOU'VE GOT EVERYTHING TO GAIN

In the previous chapters we have looked at nonverbal behaviors in various situations—primarily focusing on the employment and the performance appraisal interview. However, the nonverbal messages discussed convey cues in any situation in which there are other individuals present. The positive behaviors we have discussed will serve you well every day in other situations as well. Granted, some behaviors may be less appropriate if you find yourself operating in a culture outside North America, but otherwise our advice is to incorporate the positive behaviors into your daily routines. Doing this will serve you well. First, because you will be communicating positives in your daily routines. Second, because once you make these behaviors a normal part of your daily actions, you will automatically carry them into interview settings.

Your positive nonverbal behaviors will be your natural actions. Remember that your daily interactions with your boss and your co-workers at the office will play an important part in the outcome of the performance appraisal as well. How you conduct yourself in the appraisal interview can make a difference in the outcome, but not even the best nonverbal communications here can make up for failure to do your job or failure to communicate effectively over the entire period covered by the review. The savvy interviewer doesn't just turn on the positive nonverbal communication for the important occasions in her life; she knows every moment of every day brings important interactions with others.

Behaviors To Live By Every Day

On the following list you will find a summary of many of the positive nonverbal behaviors we have discussed in the previous chapters. You may wish to use this as a quick review list of the behaviors, which have been discussed more fully in the text. Remember that you want the interviewer to feel comfortable with you, to see that you fit into the organization, to understand that you are "one of them." Some appropriate behaviors are simply good manners.

- Convey consistent messages
  - verbal and nonverbal cues are consistent with one another
  - various nonverbal cues are consistent with one another
- Use interviewer's title and last name, and get it right
- Wear clothing that "fits in" with the organization
- Wear clothing that says "professional"
- Wear clothing that is compatible with your natural coloring
- Smile appropriately

- Wear an interested, enthusiastic facial expression

- Nod your head to signal agreement when appropriate

- Respect the interviewer's personal space—except for shaking hands about 4-6 feet apart

- Shake hands by extending yours with the palm turned upward at a slight angle and meet his hand web to web, shake once or twice and release

- When standing, keep both feet flat on the floor with your weight evenly distributed

- When seated, both feet flat on floor is best

- Take a seat after the interviewer has indicated where you should sit

- Sit in the chair with a slight forward body lean

- Establish frequent eye contact with the interviewer

- Keep your hands at or below your waist

- When standing, keep your hands at your side—unless gesturing

- When seated, keep your hands resting in your lap—unless gesturing

- Gesture naturally in a manner consistent with your message

- Be comfortable with silence; use it to your advantage

- Speak at a moderate rate

- Vary your speaking rate to emphasize an idea

- Project your voice; project your dynamism

- Vary your vocal inflection

- Convey your enthusiasm with your voice

- Pause occasionally

- Fill your pauses with silence

As you convey your competence through both your verbal and nonverbal behaviors you are perceived as an individual who will fit into the organization. Always convey dynamism. Your enthusiastic responses—both verbal and nonverbal— help you sell yourself for the position or promotion you want. Paul Tsongas, Michael Dukakis, and Bob Dole are three people who were credible and competent individuals and who achieved much in their professional lives. However, they were not able to sell themselves for the highest job in the nation in large measure because of their lack of dynamism.

> Always convey your dynamism. Enthusiastic responses—both verbal and nonverbal— help you sell yourself for the position or promotion you want.

Behaviors To Avoid

In many cases the behaviors to avoid will be the opposite of the behaviors to engage in which are on the list above. Again, you goal is to avoid behaviors that make the interviewer feel uncomfortable or make him feel that you will not fit into their corporate environment. You want to avoid behaviors that lower your credibility and hence call into question your competence to do the job.

- Do not convey inconsistent messages—your words convey that you are interested in the job but the lack of dynamism in your facial expression and voice indicate the opposite

- Do not call the interviewer by his first name (unless requested to do so) nor mispronounce the name

- Do not groom or dress yourself in a manner that will attract undue attention or make you stand apart from those individuals at high levels in the organization

- Do not sit until asked to by the interviewer

- Avoid being "too" anything—not too flashy, not too casual in your dress or manner, not too talkative, not too quiet

- Do not have a sullen, angry or disinterested facial expression

- Do not invade the interviewer's personal space

- Do not shake hands with a limp hand, nor just your fingertips, nor pump the hand incessantly

- Do not lower your eyes, unable to meet the interviewer's gaze

- Do not stare

- Do not shift your weight from one foot to the other while standing, or rock back and forth

- Do not slouch

- Do not lean back against the back of your chair

- Do not cross your legs

- Do not engage in grooming behaviors such as constantly pushing hair back or playing with your cuticles or nails

- Do not fidget with your hands

- Do not play with anything—a pen, a notepad or your clothing

- Do not pick up anything from the interviewer's desk without requesting permission

- Do not look at your watch

- Do not move your hands and arms about in wild and constant gestures

- Do not fold your arms across your chest

- Do not talk too little

- Do not talk too much

- Do not ramble

- Do not forget to pause occasionally

- Do not fill pauses with vocalized pauses or fillers

- Do not rush in to fill silence with verbiage

- Do not speak too softly

- Do not speak too rapidly

- Do not speak too slowly

Your goal is to convey that you are a competent, enthusiastic individual who can interact well with others—your boss, your co-workers, your subordinates—in order to accomplish the organization's goals. You need to convey that you can interact and do business with the company's clients. You are a go-getter who can get the job done. As you nonverbally convey your comfort, you make the interviewer feel more comfortable. He feels good about you because he feels good about the interaction with you. He perceives you to be a credible and competent person who will make a good employee!

Psych Yourself for Your Interview

Do you remember the song from **The King and I** when Anna counsels her son to *Whistle a Happy Tune*? She tells him if he'll whistle whenever he feels afraid, he'll not only fool others—he'll fool himself as well! Psychologists tell us that our minds can only hold one thought at a time. So you chose. Are you going to let your "internal critic" take over and hold negative thoughts—hold thoughts of fear and failure in your mind? Tell yourself you are going to fail? Or will you allow your "internal coach" to take the lead and fill your mind with thoughts of confidence and success?

Visualize the role you want to play—one of confidence and self-assurance—and act the part. Approach the interviewer with a confident smile and your hand extended in greeting. Walk with a purposeful stride that exudes confidence, but not arrogance. Sit slightly forward in the chair and with a very slight forward lean that says I am really interested in you, your message, this organization and the job. Speak with a voice that exudes appropriate enthusiasm and interest. Display facial expression and eye gaze that compliments your words and conveys your interest. Project your voice with an air of confidence that says I am a confident and competent individual. Confidence, but not cockiness, is your message of assurance. Cocky or arrogant people actually convey their feelings of inadequacy to those who know how to read beyond the surface of the behavior. Arrogant behavior is rude behavior and does not make the other person feel comfortable.

> Project your voice with an air of confidence that says I am a confident and competent individual. Positive behaviors are important to reinforcing your feelings of self-confidence.

Positive behaviors are important to reinforcing your feelings of self-confidence as you command your body to behave in ways consistent with your goal of appearing— as well as being—self-assured. Fill your mind with confident, positive thoughts. Carry your body as if you feel confident and positive, and you can manage to both look and feel confident and competent.

Every person who makes a living in sales knows that to make a sale he has to convey his enthusiasm for the product and get the buyer to feel the same. In the interview, you are selling yourself— your skills for the job you can do. You demonstrate to the employer your strengths as much through the manner in which you conduct yourself and relate to the interviewer, as through the skills, knowledge, and abilities you document.

The savvy interviewee is confident and competent, polished and professional in demeanor and appearance. The savvy interviewee conveys his skills and his interpersonal comfort with others. The savvy interviewee makes the other person feel comfortable. The savvy interviewee demonstrates that he fits into the organization. The savvy interviewee exudes through his nonverbal behavior that, "I am one of you". The savvy interviewee is you!

ABOUT THE AUTHORS

Caryl Rae Krannich, Ph.D. and Ronald L. Krannich, Ph.D., are two of America's leading business and travel writers who have authored more than 40 books. They currently operate Development Concepts Inc., a training, consulting, and publishing firm. Caryl received her Ph.D. in Speech Communication from Penn State University. A former Peace Corps Volunteer and Fulbright Scholar, Ron received his Ph.D. in Political Science from Northern Illinois University.

Ron and Caryl are former university professors, high school teachers, management trainers, and consultants. As trainers and consultants, they have completed numerous projects on management, career development, local government, population planning, and rural development in the United States and abroad.

The Krannichs' business and career work encompasses nearly 30 books they have authored on a variety of subjects: key job search skills, public speaking, government jobs, international careers, nonprofit organizations, and career transitions. Their work represents one of today's most extensive and highly praised collections of career and business writing: *101 Dynamite Answers to Interview Questions, 101 Secrets of Highly Effective Speakers, 201 Dyna-*

mite Job Search Letters, The Best Jobs For the 21st Century, Change Your Job Change Your Life, The Complete Guide to International Jobs and Careers, Discover the Best Jobs For You, Dynamite Cover Letters, Dynamite Resumes, Dynamite Salary Negotiations, Dynamite Tele-Search, The Educator's Guide to Alternative Jobs and Careers, Find a Federal Job Fast, From Air Force Blue to Corporate Gray, From Army Green to Corporate Gray, From Navy Blue to Corporate Gray, Resumes and Job Search Letters For Transitioning Military Personnel, High Impact Resumes and Letters, International Jobs Directory, Interview For Success, Jobs and Careers With Nonprofit Organizations, Jobs For People Who Love Travel, and *Dynamite Networking For Dynamite Jobs.* Their books are found in most major bookstores, libraries, and career centers as well as on Impact's Web site: *www.impactpublications.com.* Many of their works are available interactively on CD-ROM (*The Ultimate Job Source*).

Ron and Caryl live a double career life. Authors of 13 travel books, the Krannichs continue to pursue their international interests through their innovative and highly acclaimed Impact Guides travel series (*"The Treasures and Pleasures...Best of the Best"*) which currently encompasses separate titles on Italy, France, China, Hong Kong, Thailand, Indonesia, Singapore, Malaysia, India, and Australia. When not found at their home and business in Virginia, they are probably somewhere in Europe, Asia, Africa, the Middle East, the South Pacific, or the Caribbean pursuing one of their major passions—researching and writing about quality arts and antiques.

The Krannichs reside in Northern Virginia. Frequent speakers and seminar leaders, they can be contacted through the publisher or by email: *krannich@impactpublications.com*

Index

A

Appearance, 29
Applicants, 3
Apprehension, 1
Accessories, 58
Aggression, 79
Authority, 54

B

Barriers, 71
Behavior:
   appropriate, 114-116
   inappropriate, 117-119
   changing, 104-106
   ingratiating, 17
   positive, 120
Belts:
   men, 40
   women, 58
Blouse, 51, 55, 63
Body:
   men, 33
   women, 51
Body language, 12
Braces, 40
Briefcase:
   men, 40
   women, 57

C

Car:
   men, 34
   women, 52

Coat:
   men, 41
   women, 59
Color:
   men, 42-45
   women, 55, 60-63
Color 1, 45
Competence:
   men, 45-46
   women, 54, 63-64
Confidence, 93
Cultures, 73-74, 93

D

Deception, 83-86
Delivery, 108
Diction, 106-108
Dishonesty, 16
Dress:
   importance of, 12, 30-31
   men, 34-42
   women, 53-60
Dynamism, 82, 101

E

Enthusiasm, 15
Expectations, 30
Eye:
   behavior, 90
   contact, 16, 93-96
   movement, 12
   shifty, 16

Eyeglasses:
  men, 33, 39
  women, 51, 58-59

F
Fabric, 37
Face, 58, 95-96
Facial expression, 12, 89-92
Facial hair:
  men, 32
  women, 49
Feedback, 80
Feet, 87
Fingernails:
  men, 33
  women, 49
Fit, 53

G
Gestures, 79
Greetings, 68
Grooming:
  importance of, 30
  men, 31-34
  women, 46-52

H
Hair:
  men, 32
  women, 47-49
Handbag, 57
Handkerchief, 40

I
Image, 28-64
Impressions:
  changing, 18
  first, 12, 14
  negative, 18
Interview(s):
  decisions, 2-5
  face-to-face, 26-27

job, 1
multiple, 10
outcomes, 16-19
screening, 20-23
telephone, 20-23
video, 23-26
Interviewers:
  cues, 74
  decisions, 2
  needs, 11

J
Jewelry:
  men, 38-39
  women, 57-58
Jokes, 69

L
Language:
  body, 77-88
  paralanguage, 22
Legs, 87
Listening, 96

M
Make-up, 49-50
Men, 31-46

N
Neckties, 38
Nervousness, 69, 86
Nonfluencies, 103-106
Nonverbal:
  behaviors, 78-80
  clues, 3
  communications, 12-13
  messages, 2, 10, 13
Nonverbal Interview Quotient, 4-10
Notepad, 41, 59, 83

O

Overcoat:
  men, 41

P

Pace, 102-10
Paralanguage, 22, 97
Pauses, 106
Pen:
  men, 41
  using, 83
  women, 59
Performance review, 1, 5
Physical appearance, 12
Pitch, 100-102
Pronunciation, 107-108
Proxemics, 66
Preparation, 1

Q

Qualifications:
  defining, 4
  paper, 3
Quality, 53

R

Receptionist, 67
Reading material, 67-68
Relaxing, 70, 87
Respect, 93

S

Sabotaging, 18
Salary, 111-112
Scarves, 58
Seating, 68-72
Shirt, 33, 36-37
Shoes:
  men, 34, 37-38
  women, 52, 56
Shoulders, 79
Small talk, 17-18
Smiling, 90-92

Silence, 13, 106, 109-121
Sitting, 80-81
Socks, 38
Sofas, 70-72
Space:
  conversational, 72-73
  personal, 73-74
  physical, 73
  using, 65-76
Standing, 80
Stockings, 52, 57
Suit:
  men, 34-36
  women, 51, 54

T

Talking, 109
Telephone, 20-23
Tenseness, 82
Time, 75-76

U

Umbrella:
  men, 41-42
  women, 60

V

Verbal, 1-2
Videoconferencing, 23-26
Videotelephones, 22
Vocal:
  inflection, 12-13, 15
  projection, 12-13, 98
Voice, 97-108

W

Walking, 86
Wallet, 40
Weaknesses, 11
Women, 46-64, 92, 100

Business and Career Resources

Contact Impact Publications for a free annotated listing of resources or visit the World Wide Web for a complete listing of resources: www.impactpublications.com. The following books are available directly from Impact Publications. Complete the following form or list the titles, include postage (see formula at the end), enclose payment, and send your order to:

IMPACT PUBLICATIONS
9104-N Manassas Drive
Manassas Park, VA 20111-5211
Tel 1-800/361-1055, 703/361-7300, or Fax 703/335-9486
Quick and easy online ordering: *www.impactpublications.com*

Qty.	Titles	Price	Total
BUSINESS ESSENTIALS			
_____	101 Mistakes Employers Make and How to Avoid Them	14.95	_____
_____	101 Secrets of Highly Effective Speakers	14.95	_____
_____	The Best 100 Web Sites for HR Professionals	12.95	_____
_____	Employer's Guide to Recruiting on the Internet	24.95	_____
_____	Recruit and Retain the Best	14.95	_____
_____	Take This Job and Thrive	14.95	_____
RESUMES & LETTERS			
_____	$110,000 Resume	16.95	_____
_____	100 Winning Resumes for $100,000+ Jobs	24.95	_____
_____	101 Quick Tips for a Dynamite Resume	13.95	_____
_____	1500+ Key Words for 100,000+	14.95	_____
_____	175 High-Impact Resumes	10.95	_____
_____	Adams Resume Almanac/Disk	19.95	_____
_____	America's Top Resumes for America's Top Jobs	19.95	_____
_____	Best Resumes for $75,000+ Executive Jobs	14.95	_____
_____	Better Resumes in Three Easy Steps	12.95	_____
_____	Blue Collar and Beyond	8.95	_____
_____	Blue Collar Resumes	11.99	_____
_____	Building a Great Resume	15.00	_____
_____	Cyberspace Resume Kit	16.95	_____
_____	Damn Good Resume Guide	7.95	_____
_____	Dynamite Resumes	14.95	_____
_____	Edge Resume and Job Search Strategy	23.95	_____
_____	Electronic Resumes and Onlline Networking	13.99	_____
_____	Encyclopedia of Job-Winning Resumes	16.95	_____
_____	Gallery of Best Resumes	16.95	_____
_____	Heart & Soul Resumes	15.95	_____
_____	High Impact Resumes and Letters	19.95	_____
_____	Just Resumes	11.95	_____
_____	New Perfect Resume	10.95	_____
_____	Overnight Resume	12.95	_____
_____	Portfolio Power	14.95	_____

_____	Power Resumes	14.95 _____
_____	Prof. Resumes/Executives, Managers,	
	& Other Administrators	19.95 _____
_____	Professional "Resumes For..." Career Series	213.95 _____
_____	Quick Resume and Cover Letter Book	12.95 _____
_____	Ready-To-Go Resumes	29.95 _____
_____	Resume Catalog	15.95 _____
_____	Resume Magic	18.95 _____
_____	Resume Power	12.95 _____
_____	Resume Pro	24.95 _____
_____	Resume Shortcuts	14.95 _____
_____	Resume Writing Made Easy	11.95 _____
_____	Resumes for the Over-50 Job Hunter	14.95 _____
_____	Resumes for Re-Entry	10.95 _____
_____	Resume Winners from the Pros	17.95 _____
_____	Resumes for Dummies	12.99 _____
_____	Resumes for the Health Care Professional	14.95 _____
_____	Resumes That Knock 'Em Dead	10.95 _____
_____	Resumes That Will Get You the Job You Want	12.99 _____
_____	Savvy Resume Writer	10.95 _____
_____	Sure-Hire Resumes	14.95 _____
_____	Winning Resumes	10.95 _____

COVER LETTERS

_____	101 Best Cover Letters	11.95 _____
_____	175 High-Impact Cover Letters	10.95 _____
_____	200 Letters for Job Hunters	19.95 _____
_____	201 Winning Cover Letters for the $100,000+ Jobs	24.95 _____
_____	201 Dynamite Job Search Letters	19.95 _____
_____	201 Killer Cover Letters	16.95 _____
_____	Complete Idiot's Guide to the Perfect Cover Letters	14.95 _____
_____	Cover Letters for Dummies	12.99 _____
_____	Cover Letters that Knock 'Em Dead	10.95 _____
_____	Dynamite Cover Letters	14.95 _____
_____	Gallery of Best Cover Letters	18.95 _____
_____	Haldane's Best Cover Letters for Professionals	15.95 _____
_____	Perfect Cover Letter	10.95 _____
_____	Winning Cover Letters	10.95 _____

INTERVIEWING: JOBSEEKERS

_____	101 Dynamite Answers to Interview Questions	12.95 _____
_____	101 Dynamite Questions to Ask at Your Job Interview	14.95 _____
_____	101 Tough Interview Questions. . .	14.95 _____
_____	111 Dynamite Ways to Ace Your Job Interview	13.95 _____
_____	Haldane's Best Answers to Tough Interview Questions	15.95 _____
_____	Information Interviewing	10.95 _____
_____	Interview for Success	15.95 _____
_____	Job Interviews for Dummies	12.99 _____
_____	Savvy Interviewer	10.95 _____

NETWORKING

_____	Dig Your Well Before You're Thirsty	24.95 _____
_____	Dynamite Networking for Dynamite Jobs	15.95 _____
_____	Dynamite Tele-Search	12.95 _____
_____	Golden Rule of Schmoozing	12.95 _____
_____	Great Connections	11.95 _____
_____	How to Work a Room	11.99 _____
_____	Network Your Way to Success	19.95 _____
_____	Power Networking	14.95 _____
_____	Power Schmoozing	12.95 _____

SALARY NEGOTIATIONS

_____	Dynamite Salary Negotiations	15.95 _____
_____	Get a Raise in 7 Days	14.95 _____
_____	Get More Money on Your Next Job	14.95 _____
_____	Negotiate Your Job Offer	14.95 _____

IMAGE AND ETIQUETTE

_____	Business Etiquette and Professionalism	10.95 _____
_____	Dressing Smart in the New Millennium	13.95 _____
_____	Executive Etiquette in the New Workplace	14.95 _____
_____	First Five Minutes	14.95 _____
_____	John Malloy's Dress for Success (For Men)	13.99 _____
_____	Lions Don't Need to Roar	10.99 _____
_____	New Professional Image	12.95 _____
_____	New Women's Dress for Success	12.99 _____
_____	Red Socks Don't Work	14.95 _____
_____	Winning Image	17.95 _____
_____	You've Only Got 3 Seconds	22.95 _____

INTERNET JOB SEARCH/HIRING

_____	100 Top Internet Job Sites	12.95 _____
_____	Career Exploration On the Internet	15.95 _____
_____	Electronic Resumes	19.95 _____
_____	Employer's Guide to Recruiting on the Internet	24.95 _____
_____	Guide to Internet Job Search.	14.95 _____
_____	Heart & Soul Internet Job Search	16.95 _____
_____	How to Get Your Dream Job Using the Web	29.99 _____
_____	Internet Jobs Kit	149.95 _____
_____	Internet Resumes	14.95 _____
_____	Job Searching Online for Dummies	24.99 _____
_____	Resumes in Cyberspace	14.95 _____

ALTERNATIVE JOBS & EMPLOYERS

_____	100 Best Careers for the 21st Century	15.95 _____
_____	100 Great Jobs and How To Get Them	17.95 _____
_____	101 Careers	16.95 _____
_____	150 Best Companies for Liberal Arts Graduates	15.95 _____
_____	50 Coolest Jobs in Sports	15.95 _____
_____	Adams Job Almanac 2000	16.95 _____
_____	American Almanac of Jobs and Salaries	20.00 _____
_____	Back Door Guide to Short-Term Job Adventures	19.95 _____
_____	Best Jobs for the 21st Century	19.95 _____
_____	Breaking & Entering	17.95 _____
_____	Careers in Computers	17.95 _____
_____	Careers in Health Care	17.95 _____
_____	Careers in High Tech	17.95 _____
_____	Career Smarts	12.95 _____
_____	Cool Careers for Dummies	16.95 _____
_____	Cybercareers	24.95 _____
_____	Directory of Executive Recruiters	44.95 _____
_____	Flight Attendant Job Finder	16.95 _____
_____	Great Jobs Ahead	11.95 _____
_____	Health Care Job Explosion!	17.95 _____
_____	Hidden Job Market 2000	18.95 _____
_____	High-Skill, High-Wage Jobs	19.95 _____
_____	JobBank Guide to Computer and High-Tech Companies	16.95 _____
_____	JobSmarts Guide to Top 50 Jobs	15.00 _____
_____	Liberal Arts Jobs	14.95 _____
_____	Media Companies 2000	18.95 _____

_____	Sunshine Jobs	16.95	_____
_____	Take It From Me	12.00	_____
_____	Top 100	19.95	_____
_____	Top 2,500 Employers 2000	18.95	_____
_____	Trends 2000	14.99	_____
_____	What Employers Really Want	14.95	_____
_____	Working in TV News	12.95	_____
_____	Workstyles to Fit Your Lifestyle	11.95	_____
_____	You Can't Play the Game If You Don't Know the Rules	14.95	_____

RECRUITERS/EMPLOYERS

_____	Adams Executive Recruiters Almanac	16.95	_____
_____	Directory of Executive Recruiters	44.95	_____
_____	Employer's Guide to Recruiting on the Internet	24.95	_____

JOB STRATEGIES AND TACTICS

_____	101 Ways to Power Up Your Job Search	12.95	_____
_____	110 Big Mistakes Job Hunters Make	19.95	_____
_____	24 Hours to Your Next Job, Raise, or Promotion	10.95	_____
_____	Better Book for Getting Hired	11.95	_____
_____	Career Bounce-Back	14.95	_____
_____	Career Chase	17.95	_____
_____	Career Fitness	19.95	_____
_____	Career Intelligence	15.95	_____
_____	Career Starter	10.95	_____
_____	Coming Alive From 9 to 5	18.95	_____
_____	Complete Idiot's Guide to Changing Careers	17.95	_____
_____	Executive Job Search Strategies	16.95	_____
_____	First Job Hunt Survival Guide	11.95	_____
_____	Five Secrets to Finding a Job	12.95	_____
_____	Get a Job You Love!	19.95	_____
_____	Get It Together By 30	14.95	_____
_____	Get the Job You Want Series	37.95	_____
_____	Get Ahead! Stay Ahead!	12.95	_____
_____	Getting from Fired to Hired	14.95	_____
_____	Great Jobs for Liberal Arts Majors	11.95	_____
_____	How to Get a Job in 90 Days or Less	12.95	_____
_____	How to Get Interviews from Classified Job Ads	14.95	_____
_____	How to Succeed Without a Career Path	13.95	_____
_____	How to Get the Job You Really Want	9.95	_____
_____	How to Make Use of a Useless Degree	13.00	_____
_____	Is It Too Late To Run Away and Join the Circus?	14.95	_____
_____	Job Hunting in the 21st Century	17.95	_____
_____	Job Hunting for the Utterly Confused	14.95	_____
_____	Job Hunting Made Easy	12.95	_____
_____	Job Search: The Total System	14.95	_____
_____	Job Search Organizer	12.95	_____
_____	Job Search Time Manager	14.95	_____
_____	JobShift	13.00	_____
_____	JobSmart	12.00	_____
_____	Kiplinger's Survive and Profit From a Mid-Career Change	12.95	_____
_____	Knock 'Em Dead	12.95	_____
_____	Me, Myself, and I, Inc.	17.95	_____
_____	New Rights of Passage	29.95	_____
_____	No One Is Unemployable	29.95	_____
_____	Not Just Another Job	12.00	_____
_____	Part-Time Careers	10.95	_____
_____	Perfect Job Search	12.95	_____
_____	Princeton Review Guide to Your Career	20.00	_____
_____	Perfect Pitch	13.99	_____
_____	Portable Executive	12.00	_____
_____	Professional's Job Finder	18.95	_____

_____	Reinventing Your Career	9.99 _____
_____	Resumes Don't Get Jobs	10.95 _____
_____	Right Fit	14.95 _____
_____	Right Place at the Right Time	11.95 _____
_____	Second Careers	14.95 _____
_____	Secrets from the Search Firm Files	24.95 _____
_____	So What If I'm 50	12.95 _____
_____	Staying in Demand	12.95 _____
_____	Strategic Job Jumping	13.00 _____
_____	SuccessAbilities	14.95 _____
_____	Take Yourself to the Top	13.99 _____
_____	Temping: The Insiders Guide	14.95 _____
_____	Top 10 Career Strategies for the Year 2000 & Beyond	12.00 _____
_____	Top 10 Fears of Job Seekers	12.00 _____
_____	Ultimate Job Search Survival	14.95 _____
_____	VGMs Career Checklist	9.95 _____
_____	Welcome to the Real World	13.00 _____
_____	What Do I Say Next?	20.00 _____
_____	What Employers Really Want	14.95 _____
_____	When Do I Start	11.95 _____
_____	Who Says There Are No Jobs Out There	12.95 _____
_____	Work Happy Live Healthy	14.95 _____
_____	Work This Way	14.95 _____

ATTITUDE & MOTIVATION

_____	100 Ways to Motivate Yourself	15.99 _____
_____	Attitude Is Everything	14.99 _____
_____	Change Your Attitude	15.99 _____
_____	Reinventing Yourself	18.99 _____

INSPIRATION & EMPOWERMENT

_____	10 Stupid Things Men Do to Mess Up Their Lives	13.00 _____
_____	10 Stupid Things Women Do	13.00 _____
_____	101 Great Resumes	9.99 _____
_____	Beating Job Burnout	12.95 _____
_____	Big Things Happen When You Do the Little Things Right	15.00 _____
_____	Career Busters	10.95 _____
_____	Chicken Soup for the Soul Series	87.95 _____
_____	Do What You Love, the Money Will Follow	11.95 _____
_____	Doing Work You Love	14.95 _____
_____	Emotional Intelligence	13.95 _____
_____	Get What You Deserve	23.00 _____
_____	Getting Unstuck	11.99 _____
_____	If Life Is A Game, These Are the Rules	15.00 _____
_____	Job/Family Challenge: A 9-5 Guide	12.95 _____
_____	Kick In the Seat of the Pants	11.95 _____
_____	Kiplinger's Taming the Paper Tiger	11.95 _____
_____	Life Skills	17.95 _____
_____	Love Your Work and SuccessWill Follow	12.95 _____
_____	Path, The	14.95 _____
_____	Seven Habits of Highly Effective People	14.00 _____
_____	Softpower	10.95 _____
_____	Stop Postponing the Rest of Your Life	9.95 _____
_____	Suvivor Personality	12.00 _____
_____	To Build the Life You Want, Create the Work You Love	10.95 _____
_____	Unlimited Power	12.00 _____
_____	Wake-Up Calls	18.95 _____
_____	Your Signature Path	24.95 _____

TESTING AND ASSESSMENT

_____ Career Counselor's Tool Kit	45.00	_____
_____ Career Discovery Project	12.95	_____
_____ Career Exploration Inventory	29.95	_____
_____ Career Satisfaction and Success	14.95	_____
_____ Career Tests	12.95	_____
_____ Crystal-Barkley Guideto Taking Charge of Your Career	9.95	_____
_____ Dictionary of Holland Occupational Codes	45.00	_____
_____ Discover the Best Jobs For You	14.95	_____
_____ Discover What You're Best At	12.00	_____
_____ Gifts Differing	14.95	_____
_____ Have You Got What It Takes?	12.95	_____
_____ How to Find the Work You Love	10.95	_____
_____ Making Vocational Choices	29.95	_____
_____ New Quick Job Hunting Map	4.95	_____
_____ P.I.E. Method for Career Success	14.95	_____
_____ Putting Your Talent to Work	12.95	_____
_____ Real People, Real Jobs	15.95	_____
_____ Starting Out, Starting Over	14.95	_____
_____ Test Your IQ	6.95	_____
_____ Three Boxes of Life	18.95	_____
_____ Type Talk	11.95	_____
_____ WORKTypes	12.99	_____
_____ You and Co., Inc.	22.00	_____
_____ Your Hidden Assets	19.95	

☞ **SUBTOTAL** $ _____

☞ Virginia residents add 4½% sales tax)   _____

☞ Shipping/handling, Continental U.S., $5.00 +   _____ $5.00
plus following percentages when **SUBTOTAL** is:

    ☐ $30-$100—multiply SUBTOTAL by 8%   _____

    ☐ $100-$999—multiply SUBTOTAL by 7%   _____

    ☐ $1,000-$4,999—multiply SUBTOTAL by 6%   _____

    ☐ Over $5,000—multiply SUBTOTAL by 5%   _____

☞   ☐ If shipped outside Continental US, add another 5%   _____

☞ **TOTAL ENCLOSED** $_____

SHIP TO: (street address only for UPS or RPS delivery)

Name _____

Address _____

_____

_____

Telephone _____

I enclose ☐ Check ☐ Money Order in the amount of: $ _____

Charge $_____ to ☐ Visa ☐ MC ☐ AmEx

Card #_____ Exp: _____ / _____

Signature _____

ALSO IN THE CAREERSAVVY SERIES™:

Anger and Conflict in the Workplace
100 Top Internet Job Sites
101 Hiring Mistakes Employers Make
The 100 Best Web Sites For HR Professionals
The Difficult Hire
Recruit and Retain the Best
The Savvy Resume Writer

DISCOVER HUNDREDS OF ADDITIONAL RESOURCES ON THE WORLD WIDE WEB!

Looking for the newest and best books, directories, newsletters, wall charts, training programs, videos, computer software, and kits to help you land a job, negotiate a higher salary, or start your own business? Want to learn the most effective way to find a job in Asia or relocate to San Francisco? Are you curious about how to find a job 24 hours a day using the Internet or about what you'll be doing five years from now? Are you trying to keep up-to-date on the latest career resources, but are not able to find the latest catalogs, brochures, or newsletters on today's "best of the best" resources?

Welcome to the first virtual career bookstore on the Internet. Now you're only a click away with Impact Publications' electronic solution to the resource challenge. Visit this rich site to quickly discover everything you ever wanted to know about finding jobs, changing careers, and starting your own business—including many useful resources that are difficult to find in local bookstores and libraries. The site also includes what's new and hot, tips for job search success, and monthly specials. Check it out today!

www.impactpublications.com